Lou Vairo

Lou Vairo
The Godfather of US Hockey

Lou Vairo

with Michael McKinley

ROWMAN & LITTLEFIELD
Lanham • Boulder • New York • London

Published by Rowman & Littlefield
An imprint of The Rowman & Littlefield Publishing Group, Inc.
4501 Forbes Boulevard, Suite 200, Lanham, Maryland 20706
www.rowman.com

86-90 Paul Street, London EC2A 4NE, United Kingdom

British Library Cataloguing in Publication Information Available

Library of Congress Cataloging-in-Publication Data
Names: Vairo, Lou, author. | McKinley, Michael, 1961– author.
Title: Lou Vairo : the godfather of US hockey / Lou Vairo With Michael McKinley.
Description: Lanham, Maryland : Rowman & Littlefield, 2024. | Includes bibliographical
    references and index. | Summary: "The remarkable autobiography of Lou Vairo, the 'Godfather
    of Hockey,' who studied under the great Russian coach Anatoli Tarasov and returned to the U.S.
    to propel the game to unprecedented heights. Vairo would go on to become a scout for the gold
    medal 1980 Miracle on Ice Olympic team, head coach for the 1984 Olympic team, and NHL
    coach"— Provided by publisher.
Identifiers: LCCN 2024011185 (print) | LCCN 2024011186 (ebook) | ISBN 9781538195659
    (cloth) | ISBN 9781538195666 (epub)
Subjects: LCSH: Vairo, Lou. | Hockey coaches—United States—Biography. | Hockey—United
    States—History—20th century. | National Hockey League—History—20th century.
Classification: LCC GV848.5.V33 A3 2024 (print) | LCC GV848.5.V33 (ebook) | DDC
    796.962092 [B]—dc23/eng/20240426
LC record available at https://lccn.loc.gov/2024011185
LC ebook record available at https://lccn.loc.gov/2024011186

♾️™ The paper used in this publication meets the minimum requirements of American National
Standard for Information Sciences—Permanence of Paper for Printed Library Materials, ANSI/
NISO Z39.48-1992.

To Yuri Igorovich Karmanov, April 26, 1952–June 9, 2022

I am dedicating this book to my very best friend—to me, a brother. I was introduced by a mutual friend to Yuri Igorovich Karmanov in 1992 in Milano, Italy. Yuri was interested in being assistant coach of the team I was going to coach, Saima Milano. After a forty-minute meeting, I hired him. He was a very important part of our team that went on to become Italian champions. He would, in ensuing years, ask me and encourage me to write a book. After his passing I promised myself I would do so in his honor. He was a blessed friend, and his widow, Svetlana, remains a blessed friend to this day. Yuri, RIP my dear brother.

CONTENTS

FOREWORD

IT MAY BE HARD TO IMAGINE TODAY, BUT AS A BOY BORN IN ST. LOUIS and living there until I was seven, then growing up on the lakes of Waterford, Michigan, there were very few American-born professional hockey players to emulate. In fact, the best I ever hoped for as a teenage hockey player was to maybe one day earn a scholarship at the University of Michigan or at Michigan State, which would have been (and still is) quite the accomplishment.

The guys I grew up with in Michigan really didn't even aspire to play in Canadian Junior Hockey leagues because this just wasn't something that US-born players did back then. I always was a fan of the free-flowing game, and my early heroes were Canadians Guy Lafleur and Gilbert Perreault. Whenever the Olympics rolled around, I marveled at the team speed and grace of Russian players like Valeri Kharlamov and Boris Mikhailov. They were my size, but they could control a game with their skill and speed.

My dad worked for Chrysler in Detroit, and he served as our youth hockey coach. He always stressed that we should work on our weaknesses. We had some local success and prayed for that chance to get a college scholarship.

However, all of that began to change on the night of my fifteenth birthday—February 22, 1980. You'll remember that Herb Brooks led a bunch of college kids into the semifinal match in Lake Placid and beat the Soviets, 4–3. Suddenly, our bar had been raised a bit. Perhaps my local teammates and I could aspire to one day represent our country and play in a future Olympic Games?

If you'd told me that three years later, I'd be playing for the US Olympic Team against the Russians under Coach Lou, I would have said you were crazy. But there I was, and I consider that time one of the best times of my life. Because Lou Vairo is one of the best guys in my life.

I remember Coach Lou telling me about his travels in Russia. When Lou met Anatoli Tarasov and learned about Russian hockey from him, it was then that Lou's hockey calling found him. He saw a way to play hockey that would make us all better players.

I can tell you from my more than forty years in the game that hockey teaches you the values, character, and the lessons and life skills that you carry with you for your whole life. You learn teamwork and leadership. You learn how to overcome adversity, how to win with grace, and how to lose if you must, and so this great game really teaches you about life. Which is what Coach Lou taught me.

He just loves the game of hockey. He loves to teach, and he loves to coach. He's a born communicator and he was born to be a coach. His legacy has inspired and influenced the sport beyond what I can describe here, but Coach was essential in growing USA Hockey into the force it has become. He embodies the values of the game and the character of the game because he loves it so much and wants the world to love it too.

When we began our Olympic adventure in August 1983, we knew that we had a tall order to fill. We needed to repeat that 1980 Olympic gold. A lot of coaches refused to take up that daunting challenge to follow in Herb Brooks's winning footsteps, but Lou was not afraid to take it. He stepped up, and then he gave all of us young hotshots an education on his brand of hockey.

In the 2004 movie, *Miracle on Ice*, there is a scene in which Kurt Russell, playing coach Herb Brooks, comes in and makes the team do a bag skate, which is when your coach is trying to make a point. You can skate laps, sprint between goal lines, and just generally skate until you drop.

Well, we got a taste of that in person, as Lou had been there in 1980, and saw Brooks in action. So, when we showed up to play hockey that August, Lou reminded us that we needed to get in shape by making us do a bag skate. We skated for 45 minutes, just like in the movie. We got in shape fast.

It was Coach Lou's practices, though, that were unlike any we had seen. We did tumble rolls on the ice, for example, to improve our agility. He's the only coach I know outside of Tarasov who didn't wear hockey gloves. He wore bandy gloves, which are more compact, and from the game which is like hockey but played with a ball, and popular in Russia. Lou could take you out of your comfort zone and challenge you, but he cared about you. Lou wanted everybody to play well and to play as a team. But we knew that he cared about his players like a father.

I finally did get to play against the Russians when we played a series out in Alaska against the Soviet Wings four times, twice in Anchorage, once in Fairbanks, and once in Soldotna. We also played the Russians at Lake Placid in December 1983, and we beat them. I got a goal. It was thrilling.

After our Alaska games, Lou took the whole team to King Salmon, which is about 250 miles southwest of Anchorage and a place you can get to only by boat or seaplane. We came in on seaplanes for a few days of fishing and team bonding. We also got to see grizzly bears up close— very close, in fact—and we feasted like kings on salmon and steak. Lou wanted to make us feel like kings, and even though we didn't win gold in 1984, we had a great team, and the best coach. Sport is like that and why we love it. You win some and you lose some, but there is always your next game, or your next season, to try again.

So, too, for Lou. He is now coaching the next generation of great American hockey players in Colorado with the Colorado Rampage Youth Hockey program. With a gleam in his eye and a smile for everyone, Lou is bringing that passion for the game born from his roller hockey days on the streets of Brooklyn to those kids on the Colorado Rampage ice, teaching them how to "be" hockey players. As he has been doing, now for more than fifty years, Coach Lou is giving young hockey players the finest lessons they can learn about how to play this wonderful game. I speak for thousands of players over a few generations when I say for us all "You made me a better player, and a better person. Thank you, Coach!"

Pat LaFontaine

ACKNOWLEDGMENTS

Many people have helped us with our book, and we thank them all, especially the team at Rowman & Littlefield. We thank Dave Fischer of USA Hockey and Alexei Tarasov for providing us with photos. We thank Willie O'Ree for suggesting the book in the first place, and to David and Brenda Samsom for connecting Lou and Michael. And we want to shout our thanks to our great friend Will Cooper, for believing in this great story, and for making it happen.

Chapter 1

A Brooklyn Guy

I was born on February 25, 1945, in Kings County Hospital in Brooklyn, New York. The world was still at war, and apparently, I came into it with an attitude. My mother told me that mine was a very difficult delivery. When I made my debut, they had to drag me out with instruments. As a result, my mother said that my head was in the shape of a banana—a banana covered with black hair. She said when they put me on her stomach and she held me up to have a look at her firstborn, she cried. "No, this can't be my son," she said as tears ran down her face. "Take him away."

In a few days, the swelling on my head went down and my mother saw that I was indeed not a banana with hair but, in fact, her son. I was supposed to be named Salvatore after my father's father, but my mother said, "Hold on one second. I am going to name him after his father. This is the United States, and we don't need all these Old World names." The fact that my father was named Luigi was apparently not an issue, so I was christened as Luigi, and I very soon became Lou.

I was the eldest of what would turn out to be a family of six kids—I had two sisters and three brothers. Of course, they all worshiped me and catered to my every whim. I'm kidding. We got along, but like any family, we had our bumps along the way.

We were a typical Brooklyn family at the end of World War II. We lived in an apartment building in East New York, Brooklyn, at Winthrop and East 51st Street. We lived on the fourth floor. There was no elevator, so you would walk up this big marble staircase, lit by chandeliers. We had a kitchen, a dining room, a bathroom, two bedrooms and a living room. There were no screens or bars on the windows. We could have fallen out of them to our doom a thousand times, but we did not. It was beautiful.

I remember my father constantly complaining about how expensive the rent was. It was $40 a month and on the last Friday of every month, the rent was due. The owner of the building would knock on the door, and my mother, Elizabeth, whom everyone called Betty, would hand the rent collector four $10 bills.

My father was a milkman for a while, then delivered mayonnaise, then had a juice route that never made a lot of money, and he did some other things as well to provide for us. When I had no school in the summertime, he would have me help him, and there was never a day that I didn't either quit or he fired me. It was funny how I could wind him up, and he could get me angry. But the next day we'd go out and do it all again.

He knew everybody on the route, and he spoke a little bit of a hundred languages. We even delivered to Mario Cuomo, the future governor of New York, and his parents. Mario's mother used to make the best sandwiches. We also used to deliver juice to the mob boss Joe Colombo. My father said, "You never charge him." Mr. Colombo would say to my father, "If you ever need anything, you call me."

My father was such a good guy and so personable that he could deal with anybody, and he loved people. He was a good, kind man.

My mother was tough and strict, and she ran the show. She would call us up just once for supper, and if we didn't immediately leave the game we were playing outside, she would come down with a rolling pin in her hand to repeat the command. She never hit us, but it scared the hell out of us.

My mother was a housewife, and that's a very difficult job. You have to keep the household together, and with six kids, four of them being rambunctious boys, it's not an easy task. But she did it, and we loved her for how she did it.

On the really hot and sticky days that hit New York City in summer, the days where you need a shower as soon as you step out of the shower, she would let us sit out on the fire escape. I can't imagine now how dangerous that must have been, but nobody ever fell or jumped off. Sometimes my mother would fill up a bucket with cold water and just pour it over our heads to cool us down. We all swore we were at the beach.

We had linoleum floors in our apartment, and one day my mother was all excited because my father had bought her a rug. I was about six years old at the time, and she made me and Jerry, my next brother in line, take our shoes off. We never took our shoes off because the floor was just linoleum, but my mother insisted, as she was so thrilled by this new rug. So we took our shoes off and I was looking around for this new rug, and then finally I spotted it, a little thing that was two feet by four feet and under the coffee table. As I said, we didn't have much, and so it didn't take much to make us happy.

We had no washing machine, so my mother would wash everything in the bathtub with a scrub board, then rinse it out and hang it on the clothesline which stretched across the alley to an apartment across the way. We had that fire escape, of course, so she would put plants out there in the summer—the fresh herbs with which she would season her delicious Italian dishes.

You know, I have a fondness for those simple days. As a kid I would get a pair of shoes, inevitably a pair of sneakers, a couple of dress shirts, and school slacks, plus one pair of blue jeans. And those would be my clothes for the year. My four brothers coming after me inherited my stuff, because I was the oldest, and we didn't have a lot of money. That's just the way it was, and it was fine.

We moved to a housing project in Canarsie, Brooklyn, when I was ten years old, and I went to PS 115. The school was about a mile from where we lived, so we walked to school, no matter what season, and on the walk home we would explore empty lots, climb trees, walk on ledges, and have fights.

One morning when I was heading out to school, I saw a dead body on the sidewalk in front of our apartment building. The guy had been shot in the head over a crap game. There was a pool of blood in the chalk outline on the sidewalk where the crap game happened.

I just went on my way to school and never thought about it. That was the way it was done back then. I remember some members of my family telling me when I was little, "Don't ever tell the cops anything! You never see nothing! You don't know nothing! You weren't there."

We call that *omertà* in Italian, or rather, those guys who were in the Mafia called it that. It meant staying silent about matters that could be considered criminal, so I just stayed silent. My immediate family were not in the Mafia, but some of my relatives were, shall we say, connected.

Here's a story for you that jumps ahead a bit in time but relates to the world from which I came. My next brother, Jerry, married a woman whose family was from Sicily. They lived in Little Italy in Manhattan. One uncle would make trips to Catania, Sicily, every year with cash stuffed in a suitcase.

So the man I knew as Uncle Sonny (my brother's wife's uncle) got a call from a guy named Paulie, who ran a chop shop on Pennsylvania Avenue in Brooklyn, where they sold spare parts for cars, and crushed cars, too.

Uncle Sonny had just been released from prison after doing a twenty-year stretch, and Paulie, who was a wonderful cook, invited him for lunch at his place in Little Italy. So they ate lunch, then Paulie told Sonny he wanted to show him something outside. It was a black Lincoln Continental with Michigan license plates parked out on Hester Street.

Paulie looked around to make sure no cops were watching, and then he opened the trunk and Uncle Sonny saw that the stench that wafted out from it came from the body stashed inside the trunk, wrapped in an Oriental rug. Paulie pulled the rug back and Sonny could see that the dead man had a bullet through his forehead. He also saw that the dead man was Jimmy Hoffa.

Now Jimmy Hoffa had been the head of the powerful Teamsters Union but had run afoul of Attorney General Robert F. Kennedy and had served time in prison. In 1964, Hoffa was convicted of conspiracy and mail and wire fraud concerning his handling of the Teamsters' pension fund. He got five years in prison, to run alongside an eight-year sentence he had received earlier for trying to bribe a grand juror in a case in Tennessee. But Hoffa wasn't in prison that long. President Richard Nixon shortened Hoffa's sentence and he was released from prison in 1971.

He was barred from returning to his job as the Teamsters president through a backroom deal, and Hoffa was angry. He said he would start spilling trade secrets about how the whole Teamsters machine worked with its various partners, and this made people who had worked with Hoffa, especially those in the Mafia, very nervous.

Hoffa was supposed to have a meeting with Anthony Provenzano, a high-ranking member of the Genovese crime family in New York City, and Anthony Giacalone, an alleged player in the Detroit Mafia. It was supposed to be a peace meeting to address Hoffa's hard push to regain power, but it was not at all about peace. It was about making Jimmy Hoffa disappear from the parking lot of the Machus Red Fox restaurant in Bloomfield Township, a Detroit suburb, on July 30, 1975. And now here he was in the trunk of a car in Lower Manhattan.

Paulie told Sonny how that came to be. Paulie had been chosen, along with a guy called Chalky-Chalk, because he only wore white clothing, to go to Detroit and deal with Hoffa. They dumped their car, stole the Lincoln, and then "took care of business."

He asked Uncle Sonny to do him a favor. He needed Sonny to follow him to his chop shop and drive him back after he made Hoffa disappear forever. Paulie would pay him $500 for his time, so Sonny said yes. He drove behind the Lincoln out to Paulie's chop shop, and watched as Paulie crushed the Lincoln into a little box with dead Jimmy Hoffa inside the trunk.

Sonny said that the car leaked fluids from Hoffa's body as it was being crushed, and some dripped on his clothing, so he bought new clothes, threw the old ones in a dumpster in Chinatown, and he was, as he told me, "Good to go." He also laughed at the idea that Hoffa was buried beneath Giants Stadium, as urban legend has proclaimed. He said it was far more likely that bits of Jimmy Hoffa were in your silverware, or in the bumper of the new car you bought. That was part of my world, but not the one I grew up in.

So I went to school and kept my mouth shut and got along with everyone. We lived in the projects in Canarsie, and our neighborhood was Italian and Irish and Black and Jewish, and we all played together and respected each other. The housing project was fabulous. I learned how wonderful the diversity of our world can be, and in the end, we are all the same. It was an integrated place in every way. We never even thought about prejudice. We were all just kids.

When I came home from school I would always get called out to by a relative along the way, maybe Aunt Rose sticking her head out the window, or one of my grandmothers. They knew what time we'd come by so they would call us up on that little front porch and give us homemade breads, cookies, pizza, whatever they had made in their kitchens. I felt safe, and watched over, and loved.

When I was six or seven years old I was already sneaking off into the subway with friends, and my cousins, and sometimes with my little brother Jerry tagging along. We would get on the subway, and we didn't even know where we would go. We would run through all the subway cars to the first car and look out the front window as the train went through the tunnels as if we were standing on the bow of a magnificent vessel that would take us to the exotic lands of Queens or the Bronx. Somehow, we always made it home safely.

In summer we'd go outside after breakfast and play all day. Sometimes we didn't even come home for lunch. Nobody worried about us. It was a very different world than today.

On Sunday we went to Holy Family parish in Canarsie on Flatlands Avenue for Mass, and for some sports. The priests were very athletically inclined, and they set up the schoolyard so we could play. Monsignor Genoa strung lights up and flooded a little schoolyard about 50 feet by 50 feet so we could try ice hockey in the winter. He was out there watching us and urging us on.

And we loved sports. We played baseball in summer and hockey in winter and basketball year-round. We didn't have any equipment except that which we made, or found, or bought, like hockey sticks. The rest we had to scrounge.

We were fanatical sports fans as well. Everybody in my neighborhood, and I mean, *everybody,* was a Brooklyn Dodgers fan. I liked the Dodgers, mainly to keep the peace, but I was a Yankees fan. And I wore my Yankees cap proudly around the neighborhood. People would make me turn it around, which no one did in those days except back catchers during a baseball game. But they made me do it because nobody wanted to see the Yankees logo in Dodgers territory.

I was ten years old when the Dodgers beat the Yankees in the World Series in 1955 and my favorite player, Yogi Berra, got robbed with an amazing catch by the Dodgers' left fielder Sandy Amoros, who snagged a long ball Berra had smacked nearly out of the park. If Amoros had missed that ball, we, the Yankees, would have won the Series.

I was so pissed off. And all these people, even recent immigrants, were leaning out of their windows, banging on pots with spoons, or they were marching down the streets banging on the metal covers from garbage pails which had become cymbals. The Brooklyn Dodgers were theirs. They had won for them.

The Dodgers had won the World Series and people went wild in Brooklyn. I was upset, because if the Yankees weren't going to win it, then I wanted the Dodgers to win. But I just didn't want them to beat the Yankees to win, and that was the source of my despair.

I had been a Yankees fan since I was five years old and my father took me to a game at Yankee Stadium in the Bronx. He told me that I had to get dressed up, so I had to borrow nice clothes from my oldest cousin because I just had what I wore to school. My dad got me a little straw hat, and he was all dressed up in a nice suit with a fedora on his head. That's how you went to sporting events back then. Only a lunatic would show up in sweatpants, or face paint. And they would be looked upon, at best, with pity.

My father wanted me to see Joe DiMaggio play, as 1950 was his last year as a Yankee. We got on the subway, and we went to the Bronx. There was a big crowd at the stadium, and I had the first hot dog of my life on that day. We didn't eat hot dogs at home, but my father bought me a hot dog and a Coke. And he complained about the price, which was 40 cents for the pair. He was aggravated.

But even so, he also bought me a couple of Bryers ice cream chocolate and vanillas for 25 cents. I was only five, and I would have been happy just watching the pigeons which flew among the rafters in the bleachers where we sat. Tickets there cost 50 cents a seat. Tickets in the grandstand were a whopping $1.35. That amount is equal to $18.24 today[1] and yet the Yankees now charge $818.95 for a ticket a couple of rows up from home plate.[2] It seems if you want to study inflation, look at the cost of pro sport and concert tickets and reconcile how we got to there. I can't do it.

At that historic game in 1950, my father said, "Okay Louie, Joe DiMaggio is number five, watch him run, watch how elegant he is, how graceful he is. That's what a real athlete looks like." My father wasn't a Yankees fan, but he loved Joe DiMaggio so much that his picture was in our apartment. Along with Yogi Berra, President Truman, and Pope Pius XII. But watching Joe DiMaggio on that day turned me into a Yankees fan.

Which did not mean that I totally dismissed the Dodgers. On Saturdays I could go to a Brooklyn Dodgers game for a quarter, and I took advantage of that. Especially since before the game we got to play catch with Brooklyn Dodgers players in the outfield. About one hundred boys would show up. Not only did we play catch, but they taught us how to steal bases and how to field and how to do everything. The whole team would come out. I remember Tommy Lasorda, the left-handed pitcher, throwing balls with me. He couldn't have been nicer to us kids.

I played catch with Jackie Robinson, who was the greatest. Kind and generous, and he loved playing with us. I played catch with Carl Furillo, the six-foot-tall, 190-pound right fielder who didn't care that I was an eight-year-old kid. He was from Reading, Pennsylvania, and his nickname was "the Reading Rifle" because he could throw guys out from right field. Ebbets Field was a short field, but even so, Furillo could actually throw guys who singled to right field out at first base—his arm was that strong. I didn't like playing catch with him as my glove was not padded the way they are today, and he threw the ball painfully hard. But I realized that it was a pretty good deal, despite the pain.

We also played catch with center fielder and future Hall of Famer Duke Snider. And with the catcher, and future Hall of Famer, Roy Campanella. These guys were the best. They were part of the community of Brooklyn. They didn't make a lot of money, so we would see them riding the subway. Everybody loved the Dodgers, even me. When the Yankees weren't playing them.

Ebbets Field was an intimate place to watch a game, and it was full of characters. There was a person who rang these bells during the games, and there was a band that couldn't play a note of music, but they were a local bunch of guys from Brooklyn, and they were called the Dodgers Symphony. It was very Brooklyn, with a sense of humor about it all, and so you can see when the Dodgers actually won the World Series why it was such a big deal.

In fact, despite my Yankee pinstriped heart, one of the saddest days of my life was when the Dodgers left Brooklyn for Los Angeles in 1957, about the same time the New York Giants left for San Francisco. That left the Yankees as the only team in town until the Mets came along in 1962. But I felt bad for my friends, and I felt bad for myself every time I passed by Ebbets Field.

However, I had hockey to take my mind off it all. I was probably about ten years old when I became a Rangers fan. If we were lucky, we would get a game a week on television, and we loved it. We also played it. After a fashion.

My father's uncle was a shoemaker, so he'd get all the heels from old shoes, and he would file them down and make them round so we had pucks. Wooden sticks cost 75 cents in those days. We didn't have roller skates, so at first, we would play on our skateless feet. We would use the manhole covers in the streets as our goals, and play between them, all the while dodging traffic. Canadian players think they're tough because they have to dodge 220-pound defensemen, but we had to dodge delivery trucks, and they didn't surrender. It was a blast.

When we finally got roller skates, we played on asphalt behind a ShopRite supermarket. One day an old beat-up car drove by with a rope holding one of its doors closed. One of the windows was covered with plastic, held on with duct tape. On the side of this jalopy a sign said "A-1 Pest Control" and the guy who was driving this beast got out and asked what we were doing.

"We're playing hockey!" we told him, and he said that these conditions in the supermarket parking lot were not good for hockey. He looked at me, and took my stick, and asked why I had so much tape on it. I told him I had put it on thick so that it wouldn't break, and he shook his head. He told me that the tape makes it too heavy. "You only want it on the blade."

His name was Eddie Eskanzi. He came from a Sephardic Jewish family, by way of Spain, who ended up in Turkey during the Spanish Inquisition, and finally emigrated to New York. We didn't know it then, but he was an excellent roller hockey player. In fact, he was the Gordie Howe of Brooklyn roller hockey.

He showed us how to lift the puck, which, for us, was the heel of the shoe. He showed us how to shoot properly. Every few days he would stop by and check on us, and one day he put on his skates and whizzed around, and we were all impressed. He told us that there was a roller hockey league that we should play in, but to get there, we were going to have to take three buses.

We put on all our equipment and would get on the bus with our skates, then we'd drop 15 cents into that little container next to the bus driver and we'd make our transfers and then arrive at the outdoor rink. It had smooth asphalt and it had boards, all put together by people in the community. And they let us into their league, and so we became the Canarsie Rangers.

We loved it. We couldn't wait for Saturday. If it rained or snowed and we couldn't play, it was just horrible. It just destroyed our weekend. But when we did play, it was wonderful. We'd get on the buses in our full equipment and the bus drivers never got mad that we were bringing these hockey sticks onto their buses. They were nice people all around, and so that's how I got started. I had no ice rink to play in, so I played roller hockey.

I was also a Rangers fan, and we'd go to the old Madison Square Garden at West 49th Street and Eighth Avenue to watch the Blueshirts. It was an old building, with a Nedick's downstairs in the lobby (the Starbucks of 1950s New York, it has been called[3]), which had the best breakfast in New York City at the time. For 25 cents you could get a cup of coffee and a donut. The hot dogs came on square buns and they were delicious.

We had a card called the GO, which was an acronym for "general organization in school and in high school." You could join that club for

25 cents and with that magic GO card you could get into baseball and basketball and hockey games for 50 cents.

So I would go to games with my brother Jerry, who was two years younger than me, along with some of my friends. We'd sit in Madison Square Garden for 50 cents. We didn't even need the 30 cents for the subway, as we always snuck our way on board. We would walk about a mile to the 14th Street BMT subway in Canarsie and just wait for the right timing. That was the last stop. So we had to time it right.

We would run through the gate or under the turnstile, and the guy in the booth would holler "Hey you kids!" and blow a whistle. We just kept running onto the subway and would be on our way to Manhattan for free. We had to do it because we didn't have the money. Or we had to save what money we had for hockey.

Once we got inside MSG we had restricted seating, as you couldn't see all of the ice from the side balcony where we had to sit. But we would try to move down, because in those days, the Rangers would average 7,000 or so spectators. The Rangers weren't very good in the old Six Team NHL, and I know that it was arranged to keep them on the bottom due to the better farm systems that other teams had, and so down they stayed. They hardly ever made the playoffs, though in the mid-1950s, they did make it to the semi-finals a couple of times.

We weren't even in our seats yet before the game, and the crowd would already be chanting "Muzz must go!" Muzz Patrick was the coach and general manager of the team and was also the son of the hockey god Lester Patrick. He had won the Stanley Cup playing for the Rangers in 1940, and had taken over as GM in 1955, and he also coached them that season, and a couple of others, and those were not exactly glorious seasons as the Rangers didn't make the playoffs with him behind the bench. The fans even had balloons with "Muzz must go" painted on them and they would release these balloons in the arena, and they would swirl above Muzz Patrick and everyone else. They were wicked fans.

The most expensive seats in the Garden were the cushioned seats in the front row, right against the plexiglass. They were $4 a seat, and so far out of realm we could only gape in wonder. There's no way we could ever afford that.

But we loved our Rangers. Over my years as a ticket holder, I really got to know the hockey skills of Rod Gilbert, Jean Ratelle, and my favorite, Harry Howell. I got to meet Harry when he was scouting after his NHL career. I'd run into him often during the year, and he was a good man. So was the Rangers goalie, Gump Worsley. I got to know him later, as well, but I had no idea that would happen when I was watching him face down shooters at the Garden.

When I first took on my paper route, I was able to afford to go to two or three Ranger games a month. I delivered the *Journal American*, the *New York Times*, *Il Progresso*, and the *Daily Forward*. *Il Progresso* was an Italian paper, and the *Daily Forward* was a Jewish paper written in Hebrew. I also delivered the *New York Mirror*, and the *New York Daily News*, and I had to memorize who got what. One of the customers I delivered to in the Bayview Housing Project in Canarsie was Mr. Schultz and his family, which included his son Howard Schultz who would go on to found Starbucks.

I think it cost a customer 30 cents a week to get the paper delivered. It was hard work, but I had to do it, and I did it seven days a week. Sunday was brutal, because the newspapers are so thick and heavy on Sunday. And then I had to collect for my services. I was thrilled when I got a nickel tip. The Schultzes never tipped me, as they were poor, along with about half of my customers who never tipped me either. At the end of a good week, I might have made two bucks, or maybe two and a quarter. I had to pay room and board to my mother at 50 cents. And I had to give the church money in an envelope, as Monsignor Genoa sent me fifty-two envelopes every year for every week I had to put 50 cents in that envelope for the good works at Holy Family parish. That was $1 gone. And so I had a buck and a quarter left over. For hockey.

I have had the good fortune to meet many famous people in my life, and the first one I met was John F. Kennedy. He was running for president in 1960 and I was fifteen years old when he came to Holy Family Church to speak. I had to meet him, so I just dashed under the police barricade. The cops tried to grab me, but it was too late. I ran up to the car, and JFK was sitting in the back seat of a convertible, waving.

I shook his hand, and I can remember the sensation to this day. It was the fattest hand I have ever shaken. My father explained to me later that Kennedy's hand was puffy because he shook hands all day long. I looked in JFK's eyes, and he looked at mine, and he smiled. I said, "Just so you know, my whole family's gonna vote for you, Senator. Good luck."

"Thank you," he said, still looking me in the eye and smiling. "Thank you." He couldn't have been nicer.

Of course, he would soon be president, and then he would be dead. And I would be in the army, and maybe on my way to the war in Vietnam, the war that might not have happened if he had lived. But that's another story.

CHAPTER 2

Army Life

AFTER I LEFT HIGH SCHOOL, I WENT TO BROOKLYN COMMUNITY COLlege to study hotel management. I thought that it would be a good career for me as people are always traveling, and they always need a place to stay. I had grown up in a big family that knew how to be hospitable to strangers. So I figured hospitality was in my DNA.

Phil Chiaperini was one of the cooking instructors for our hotel management class. We had to learn some basics about food preparation, and about ordering food if we were going to successfully manage hotels. Phil asked me if I wanted a part-time job working in a restaurant on Staten Island. I said yes.

Felice's restaurant was a traditional red-and-white-checkered-tablecloth Italian restaurant at Highland Boulevard and Jefferson Avenue on Staten Island. The bar was on the left as you walked in, and the kitchen was in back, and it had booths along the side, and tables in the middle. The family who owned it lived in a house across the field out back.

They were wonderful. The grandmother lived with them, Mrs. Amante, who was from Messina, Sicily. She used to tell me that Messina was called *piccolo Parigi* or "little Paris" but everyone had left after the big earthquake in 1908 that destroyed the city and killed more than 75,000 people.[1] The survivors were moved to other cities in Italy, and many were shipped to New York, which is how Mrs. Amante, who had been a kid at the time, wound up on Staten Island.

They spoke Italian in the restaurant and Mrs. Amante always spoke to me in Italian. She could speak English, but she preferred to speak our language and I could understand it. Or most of it. She told these dramatic stories about how she managed as an immigrant. She had a daughter, and lost her husband at a young age, so she had been a single parent and it had not been an easy journey, but she was strong.

I was a skinny kid and she worried about me. She would always say "*Mangia! Mangia!*" which means "eat" and she would sneak up behind me and pat me on the face and then hand me something she had put together in the kitchen, some baking or some pasta, to try to fatten me up. She was a sweet lady.

I started out washing dishes, and then I became one of the cooks. I had grown up surrounded by Italian cooks, so I knew my way around an Italian menu. I could make pizza, pasta, or veal scallopini, whatever the customers wanted. I worked there six days a week, and I made $60 a week. I had to pay for my hotel management course, but I was still living at home, so I made do.

I would go every day to the restaurant from Canarsie in Brooklyn, which was a bit of a journey. I would take the 42 Rockaway Parkway bus to the subway, then I would take the subway to Hoyt and Schermerhorn in downtown Brooklyn, and change trains. I would take the next subway line into Manhattan to Union Square, and then change trains again and take the subway to South Ferry. Then I would walk a block to get on the Staten Island ferry, which was a ride that cost a nickel and which I loved. You sail out into New York Harbor, with Brooklyn on one side and the Statue of Liberty on the other. It's perfect on any kind of day.

Once I got to Staten Island I would take a bus which dropped me right off in front of the restaurant. I would work until about 4 p.m., and then go home, and at night I would go to my classes at Brooklyn Community College. It was about a two-hour trip each way, if everything clicked. Sometimes it was longer.

I kept my Saturdays free so I could play roller hockey, but if they needed me at Felice's on a holiday or weekend, I would work. And I didn't mind any of the work. I learned how to open clams. I learned the wisdom of using all authentic ingredients. I learned how important it was to keep the restaurant and the kitchen clean. I learned that we did not cheat customers. And Frank, the boss, taught me that the customer is always right. Almost always.

One Sunday night they were short a waiter. We had Vincenzo from Italy cooking that night, and he was good, so Frank told me that he needed me on the floor to handle table service. "I know you know how to do that," he said. "And Vincenzo will have to manage the kitchen with grandma. They'll be fine."

So I was a waiter. The restaurant was pretty high end for its time and was frequented by doctors and lawyers and people of that social strata. The night I made my debut as a waiter, this doctor came in with his wife and they sat in a booth. I had seen them in the restaurant before, but I had no interaction with them as I was in the kitchen. Tonight I was their waiter.

They ordered pasta with garlic and oil, *spaghettini aglio e olio*. So I brought the ticket in and told Vincenzo what I needed. They both wanted salad as well, so I brought them salad and bread, and another bottle of wine. The doctor was already a little drunk as he started on the second bottle, and the more he drank, the nastier he became—very demanding, wanting this and that. His wife was now becoming upset with him, but she wouldn't, or couldn't, stop him.

I remembered what Frank had told me about the customer always being right, so I brought out their beautifully prepared pasta, piping hot, and put it in front of them. Then I went off to attend to the other tables that I was serving. Suddenly I heard a whistle. This doctor was whistling at me. He said, "Hey buddy, c'mere."

I went over and said, "Yes sir, how can I help you?" He said, "What's this shit?" He was pointing at the little pieces of garlic in the dish, which are supposed to be present in oil and garlic pasta. He told me that he didn't want the dish. I asked him if he wanted me to bring him just pasta with oil. He said, "No, I want garlic and oil, but I don't want to see the garlic."

I went to the bar and spoke to Giovanna, who was a manager. I told her what happened. And she called Frank who was taking a rest. Frank knew the guy, and started talking to him, and quickly saw that he was drunk. He brought the plate back into the kitchen and came back to speak to me. I was upset.

Then the grandmother, Mrs. Amante, came out of the kitchen with a wooden spoon in hand. She spoke in Italian to Frank and said that this guy was very rude and that he had been very disrespectful to Lou. Then she told Frank to ask him to leave. "Don't charge him for anything. Tell him to go."

Frank had preached the creed that the customer was always right, but he knew on that night that he was going to have to break with his faith a bit. He looked at the doctor and his wife and told them that this situation was becoming embarrassing, and now had the attention of everyone in the restaurant. He told them that the dish that the good doctor ordered was the dish he got, and Lou, the waiter, had brought it fresh from the kitchen to him. He said that I had tried to be polite and helpful, and the doctor's wife agreed that I had, and so Frank said that maybe the doctor "should come back another time. When you're in a better frame of mind."

He didn't want to say, "Come back when you're sober," but Mrs. Amante, the grandmother, had no such compunction. She shouted out in broken English, "Maybe you come here when not drunk. Now, go away! Get out!" She really wanted to crack him over the head with that wooden spoon.

The doctor remained nasty, and he said, "I don't want my money back!" and then he threw a $100 bill on the table and left. Frank smiled at me and said, "You got a nice tip, Lou." I told him that I didn't want the money. I just didn't want to be spoken to like that. So Frank ran out and gave the $100 bill to the wife, and we never saw them again.

Frank told me that I had done well, and had handled it correctly, but I told him that I was done working the floor. "I want to go back to the kitchen, I'm safer there," I told him. The grandmother agreed, and said, in Italian, that I was to work with her in *la cucina* and nowhere else. And so I did, until 1966, when I got my notice that the US Army wanted me to work with them.

I remember telling my mother that I had been drafted into the army. She said, "Oh, I'm so proud of you. That's fantastic. You know, your dad served in World War II and all your uncles served in World War II and the Korean War. And we're so happy and so proud that our family has been able to do something for our country. We're lucky we live here." And she put her hand on my shoulder, then gave me a hug and a kiss on the cheek. And then she said, "Don't worry, you'll be safe. God only takes the good. You'll be wonderful."

I wasn't stupid. I read the newspapers, and I watched the news. I saw that the US Army was getting more involved in Vietnam. In 1965, the United States launched its first military offensive in the country even though US troops had been there for a while, and things were only escalating.[2] I knew that Vietnam was where I was most likely going to wind up.

At my first draft meeting at Whitehall Street in Lower Manhattan, the military guys running the show picked five of us, and I was one of them. They said, "We need marines. You guys are going to go into the marines. The rest of you are going into the army." I didn't know the difference between the army and the marines, so I didn't make any distinction.

However, I couldn't pass the physical for the marines. I can't touch my shoulder with my left hand. I had broken two bones in my forearm, which I had done while playing baseball, when I had run into a foul pole. The ball was sailing out of the park, and I put my glove hand up to catch the ball and instead smacked it straight into the foul pole and snapped two bones in my arm.

It didn't heal correctly, so I could never touch my left shoulder, and to this day I still can't. They would not accept me into the marines because of that injury, so they sent me back to the army.

I had to go through the army physical and they didn't see my hand-shoulder touching as any kind of impediment to military service, and so, I was in the army. However, on the day I was to report for duty in January 1967, there was a complete public transportation strike in New York City. And we did not own a car.

So I left Canarsie at 3 a.m. to be on time for my 7 a.m. appointment on Whitehall Street. And all I had with me were the bare necessities in a little bag. I had a toothbrush, toothpaste, a comb, and a razor. I wore brand-new shoes that I had bought from Thom McAn. I walked the eight and a half miles from Canarsie to Manhattan, and crossed over the Brooklyn Bridge in the freezing dark, and then arrived at Whitehall Street a little early. And by the time I got there, my new shoes were useless. I had worn out their soles on my walk.

The army put us all on a train at Grand Central Station and then we were on our way to Washington, DC. I had only been to New Jersey once in my life and I had gone to Toronto on a bus trip when I was in the Ranger fan club, but other than that, I had never left Brooklyn.

Going to Washington on the train was like going to a foreign country. And then it got even more foreign, for once we arrived in Washington, DC, we had to change trains, and I was now on my way to Fort Jackson, South Carolina. I was weary from my freezing nighttime walk from Canarsie to Manhattan, but I was sitting up all the way to South Carolina as there were no beds on this train. So I didn't sleep.

We arrived and we got issued our army boots and clothing. I was glad to see those boots, as I had to throw my new shoes away. It was a miserable first week. They picked us at random to do chores, and I had to do some painting. The paint was enamel-based and the job was indoors with turpentine as the thinner because they didn't have latex paint, which had yet to be invented. We had to keep the brushes clean with the turpentine, which I could feel burning in my lungs. It was brutal.

A few guys were sent home. One guy made Nazi symbols and said how much he hated Jews and Blacks and Indians, and another guy would pee in his bed every night. They both got out of the army by doing stuff like that. Now, 99.9 percent of the guys did not do it. But it was tempting.

You're just like a herd of animals in the army, with every facet of your being controlled by them. Where to go, what to do, when to eat. And the food was terrible. The sleeping conditions were terrible. It was not fun. But then we moved on.

For the first time in my life, I got on an airplane. It was a propeller plane that flew us to Fort Sill, Oklahoma. It was better in Oklahoma because we got put into barracks, and we were assigned to our units and then we began our basic training. It was hard, but I was lucky in that I was with a group of guys from New York, and I even knew one of them a little bit. We spoke the same language. We were comfortable with each other as we did our basic training, which wasn't too bad.

I was young and athletic and aside from that arm injury, I could do what they asked—run, jump, climb, dodge live fire, and so on. I was in the best shape of my life. I could shoot a rifle, and use a bayonet, and I had learned hand-to-hand combat. The discipline was incredible. They broke any lingering attitude in me in about three days. There was no lollygagging. It was "Yes, sir. No, sir." They beat the crap out of you in those days if you didn't do it right.

I was then sent to an artillery unit that was supposed to go to Vietnam. Sergeant Dobbs, a tough dude, who had been a prisoner of war in Korea, told us stories about how he had been treated in captivity and it was just nightmarish and gross. He told us that it was not going to be any prettier in Vietnam, but that it wouldn't be as cold as it had been in Korea. And he said that we had to be ready for everything and that they had trained us well. So we were ready.

However, one morning we were all lined up and the sergeant said, "I need somebody who knows how to cook. We got 350 hungry recruits here. They're gonna have breakfast in 45 minutes, and all the cooks on the entire base are out with flu or meningitis. Does anybody have cooking experience?"

Nobody raised their hand. I didn't either, even though I knew how to cook. The idea of cooking for 350 troops was daunting. The sergeant kept asking, and he said, "Guys we have to feed you or you're gonna go hungry. Does anybody have experience in the kitchen? Anybody?" Finally, out of the sense of putting food in my own stomach, I raised my hand. The sergeant never got my name right. He always called me "V-a-r-i-o." He said, "Atta boy, Private Vario." He pointed to ten other guys and said, "These are your helpers. Get to the kitchen. You have 40 minutes to get breakfast ready."

I didn't even know how to get into the kitchen, so first I had to find the entrance. Once inside, I did a quick run through of everything I hated about breakfast in the army. It was cold in Oklahoma in January and February, so the metal trays that they put the chilly runny eggs, and undercooked bacon and half-toasted toast on, were cold, too. I had criticized breakfast to the other guys, and we had a hard time eating it, which is tough if you're going to go do physical training and labor all day. It is, after all, the most important meal of the day.

But my time at Felice's had served me well. The first thing I did was figure out how the ovens worked. I told the guys who were helping me to get the ovens to 200 degrees and put the metal serving trays in the oven to get them warmed up. I didn't want them piping, I just wanted them to be warm enough so that when we served breakfast the guys could handle the trays as they got their food.

I told my assistant to break eight eggs in salad bowls, so we'd be ready to do what the guys wanted when they came in for breakfast. I would run the grill. I added a little garlic and onion to the meat in this huge pot in which you could cook for the masses. I added a little nutmeg to it, along with some salt and pepper, and I made a white sauce using flour and butter. I then added the milk and mixed it all together. It was pretty damn good to serve over toast. In the army it was called "shit on a shingle."

I told the guys at the toasting machine to turn up the heat a little bit as the toast has to be toasted no matter if it is white bread or brown, and we put the bacon on trays and baked it in the oven instead of frying it. We didn't have paper towels, but we had napkins, so we would drain the bacon on the napkins.

Potatoes are easy to do, and especially so then as they were already peeled from the day before. I had my guys slice them up thin and fry them with some onions and a couple of red peppers. Then we added some salt, pepper, and paprika.

We had everything going when the guys came in for breakfast, but they thought I was kidding when I asked them, as they came through the line, "Do you want your eggs over easy, over medium, or over well. Maybe scrambled? Or an omelet?"

They couldn't believe it and when they saw that I meant it, they were overjoyed. They got exactly what they wanted on warm trays in half the time it normally took to dish out breakfast. And they loved it. I didn't follow any army recipes. I knew how to cook.

I was, however, short of some herbs. I had pizza one night in this restaurant in Lawton, Oklahoma. I visited with the owners, and they told me they were originally from New Jersey. So I called up Pasquale at the pizza joint and asked if he had any fresh rosemary. And some real butter. I told him that I would give him two pounds of margarine for every pound of butter that he could provide. I needed butter to make proper gravy and other things. So I made a deal with him. I would also give him two hundred free eggs, and everyone was happy.

Especially the troops. They ate well and loved the food, and I have to say that it was delicious. However, after three days the regular cooks came back. We were all lined up outside the barracks in the freezing cold and Sergeant Dobbs said that he wanted to make an announcement. He said, "Private Vario, E1, you are being promoted to enlisted man E2. And you'll get about $8 a month more salary with that promotion. I want to thank you for what you have done."

I raised my hand and said, "So what about my ten colleagues, Sergeant? Who did 90 percent of the work? I was the orchestra leader. They were the orchestra. What about them? They get promoted too, right?"

Sergeant Dobbs said no, that Captain Good had only seen fit to promote me. So I asked the Sergeant if I could see Captain Good. I told Dobbs that I couldn't accept a promotion if the guys who made it happen don't get promoted with me. It wouldn't be right. He had a big smile on his face and told me that Captain Good would arrive at eight o'clock and that I would meet with him. Dobbs said, "I like that idea, Private. I like that."

So I met with Captain Good, who, to my surprise, did not come down all rules and order on me. He loved the idea as well, and agreed to it. I was happy and all the guys were happy, and people appreciated us even more. I knew from my time at hotel management college and Felice's and just growing up in Brooklyn that people want to eat well. Funny that the biggest thing the troops loved was the fact that the metal trays on which we served the food were warmed up. It was a sign of respect for the food and for the diners.

The next day Captain Good called me in to see him. He began, "Private First Class Vario—" and I interrupted him, and I said, "It's pronounced Vie-row, sir, or even Vay-row, but I know a Paul Vario in Brooklyn and he's a mafioso, and we're not related."

He smiled and corrected himself and said, "Well, Private Vairo, you're not going to Vietnam. Your orders have been changed. You're going to a five-day cooking school in Fort Dix, New Jersey."

I was so happy that I was going to be close to home, but he told me that I would just be in Fort Dix for a few days, and then I would be dispatched to Germany. I didn't want to leave my friends, but he told me that I had no choice. He had my orders in hand, and I would go. "They need cooks in Germany and you're ready to do it."

So I went to Fort Dix to do this mandatory five-day course and they taught me useless things like how to make mashed potatoes. It was a waste of time and space. Then they sent me to Germany. I remember we landed in Frankfurt and took the train to Heidelberg. And they picked us up in military trucks and took us to the base.

I didn't know what to expect. I knew about Hitler and the Nazis and how Germany had gone along with his crimes, and my arrival was only twenty years after the end of World War II. Germany was still rebuilding.

I would work every day with a group of German women who were dishwashers and prep cooks. I didn't know what to expect from the Germans after hearing all the stories about them and what they did to the Jews, and I brought it up in conversation. And they were ashamed. But we got along, and I made friends with some of them who remain my friends today.

One day I walked into the Café Hasler in Schwetzingen, which was about a mile from the base, with a friend of mine. We ate a German cheesecake that was very tasty. It was made with quark, which is a soft cheese used in classic German cheesecakes. But I had never heard of it before.

The cake was so delicious that I told the waitress to please offer my compliments to the baker. She went in and told him, and the baker turned out to be the owner of the café. He came out and he spoke a little English. I told him that I would love to learn how to bake the way that he baked. And he surprised me. He told me that if I could come to his café at midnight, three nights a week, he would teach me how to bake. He didn't have the money to pay me, but he said that he would give me some bread or some cakes to bring back to the base.

I have always worked. I had a paper route starting when I was twelve years old. I've never been rich, but you don't need that much to be happy. You need a nice roof over your head and good food. I just wanted to have enough money so that I could be independent and I could help others. Work did not scare me.

So I went to work at the café at night and rode there on a bicycle, which I borrowed from a Turkish guy who I knew from the base. It had a light on it and a bell to keep me visible in the dark, and so I biked the mile into town to learn German baking—and I was really keen to learn how to make German pastries.

I was also learning to speak German, and I wound up speaking it pretty well. I would work six hours, until six in the morning, and then come back and start my shift at the base, three days a week. I learned a lot about German baking and how to make those delicious pastries, and I make them to this day.

I also fell madly in love with a girl from Sicily I met in Germany. I went out with her five or six times. Back in those days, especially dating Italian girls in Europe, you were never alone with your boyfriend or your fiancé until you were married. So we were always chaperoned. As a result, our relationship never got serious, but I would have married her, if she had been willing to come to the United States. Which she was not. So I wound up marrying someone else, but that story comes later.

I came home from my military service in January 1968, sound of mind and body, as my mother had predicted. I returned to "normal" life, which was a lot more normal for me than for guys who had been fighting in the jungles of Vietnam. I got a job, and I went back to hockey, and I tried to figure out what I would do with my life. I had no idea that hockey would become my life. And that it would do so in a way that I could never have imagined when I sat up in the cheap seats in Madison Square Garden.

CHAPTER 3

Coach Lou

WHEN I CAME BACK FROM THE ARMY YOU MIGHT THINK THAT, LIKE SO many guys returning from service, I had to start all over, but in truth, I picked up pretty much where I left off. And that was thanks to the Greater New York City Ice Hockey League, which still exists, and which was born in 1967, because I was there at its birth. Sort of.

When I came back from Germany, I went to work for Bart Grillo, who played roller hockey, and that's how I came to know him. He had an air conditioning company in Brooklyn, and he worked out of his mother's garage, though he didn't live there. He was married with three daughters, and he lived in a house with them, but he ran his business out of the garage of this nice immigrant lady from Sicily. I installed air conditioners for Bart.

He told me that they were trying like hell to get an ice rink in Brooklyn, which we would eventually do, and which today is known as the Abe Stark Ice Rink on Coney Island. But prior to that, the first ice rink that we set up was through the City of New York's Parks Department in Flushing Meadows, Queens.

It was in the administration building for what had been the World's Fair, which had taken place in 1964. They held the ice theater in that building for the World's Fair, but it was a horrible building for hockey.

The distance from the ceiling to the ice surface was probably 150 feet, and the ceiling was painted entirely black. There were fifty individual white light bulbs hanging from it to mimic stars in the heavens. Instead of putting in real lights, they left these fake stars to light it. Which they did not do.

The rink was almost as wide as it was long—160 feet long and 100 feet wide. There were no boards, but it was surrounded by a concrete wall, about six feet high. Boards have give when you get checked into them, but concrete does not.

And there was no Zamboni. There were four guys who would come out every morning in a Jeep with chains on its wheels, and which featured a big triangular shaped blade that shaved the ice. One guy would drive the Jeep and the other three guys on skates would hold on to the back and guide the blade that would scrape the ice. After they had smoothed out the ice, they used a fire hose to douse the rink with water, and then they would let it set. Then we could play.

There were no benches, either, for the players to sit on. Instead there was a three-step stairway with rubber matting on its steps, and railings on the side of the stairs, on which the players would sit. And there was no door between the rink and the staircase.

Even so, we thought it was Madison Square Garden. We were so thrilled to be there that none of the place's shortcomings were a problem. I was still in the army when it was just getting started, but they made me part of the founding group, even though I wasn't there yet physically. The other founders were Bart Grillo, Eddie Eskanzi, Jerry Rodelli, Joe LaGatutta, Walter Yaciuk, Bob Ciota, and Fred Weber. It sounds like we were a Mafia group. They were just good guys who loved hockey and who wanted to help kids. They were mostly former roller hockey guys.

We produced a lot of good players, but we could only take them so far, at first. Most of our good talented players ended up going to Canada to play Junior B or Major A hockey in the Canadian junior leagues because they wanted to be professional hockey players, and there weren't many options to go to once it was time to leave us.

When we began, we figured we could handle 350 kids. And on the first day of registration, we had 380 kids sign up. Most of them could play hockey, but some of them couldn't skate well enough yet. They had played roller hockey, and they wanted to give ice hockey a shot. That's why they all joined.

Our cofounder Walter Yaciuk was a top administrator with IBM up in Westchester County, and he was a very intelligent man. He organized all our meetings. He was our secretary and treasurer, and he knew what he was doing. He had five boys, and they all played, and they were good players.

Walt said, "We have to have a mission statement." And we all looked around. We didn't know what the hell a mission statement was. So he said, "What's our goal? What are we trying to do?" Bart Grillo was a great, simple man who ran an air conditioning company, the son of Italian immigrant parents, and he said, "We want to help kids. We just want to give a chance to any kid who wants to try ice hockey to play."

So Walter replied that this was a good place to begin, but on the first day of registration our fledgling league went over our limit by thirty kids. And Bart said, "I don't care if we go over by 500 kids, we'll figure it out. We're not going to turn anyone away. That's our mission statement." And that's what we did.

I used to run hockey clinics on the outdoor rink in Central Park. I often would see Black kids or Hispanic kids watching the practice or the game because the rink is at the northern part of Central Park, right between Harlem and Spanish Harlem.

I would skate over to the sideboard and ask them if they wanted to try to play the game. Some of them couldn't even speak English, but they all conveyed that yes, they would love to give it a try. I told them that it cost $15 to join the League, and that they would have to come to Flushing, Queens, to get into our league.

Then we had a meeting with all the parents and kids in our league, and we asked if they would be interested in collecting used hockey equipment, making any necessary repairs, and cleaning it up, to help those kids who were less fortunate to have a chance to play hockey. Of course, the answer was a resounding yes and so we continued our mission. All of a sudden, we all found ourselves polishing skates with cleaning spray, and using Lysol to clean equipment. If the kids couldn't afford the $15 fee, we waived it.

So we got all these kids coming to Queens from northern Manhattan, and there were some really good players. I remember Hector and

Eddie Rivera, talented players who are grandfathers today. Hector retired as a distinguished fireman and Eddie is currently a world champion ballroom dancer. And it became generational. These kids played, then their kids played, and now they take their grandkids to the rink to play.

We had all levels, from mites and squirts to peewee and bantam to midgets and juveniles. Then we landed a junior team in the New York Metropolitan league that was started by Emil Francis, the legendary New York Rangers player, coach, and general manager. We had three teams in the Met league: the Shamrocks, the Brooklyn Stars, and the Manhattan Skyliners.

Emil Francis came to New York, and he changed everything. I got to become very good friends with Emil, and his son Bobby would one day play for me. This little guy from North Battleford, Saskatchewan, had been a wonderful goalie for the Chicago Black Hawks and then the Rangers. He changed many lives for the better, and he did more for hockey in New York than anybody. I mean, I would not be speaking to you today if it wasn't for Emil.

Many years later I recommended that he receive the Wayne Gretzky International Award for his contributions to hockey in the United States. He was so thrilled, and at the time he was in his late eighties. Since he had also coached the Rangers, a lot of ex-Rangers had come out to honor the man they had called Emil "The Cat" because his reflexes were so quick.

At the Gretzky Award Emil looked just like he looked in the 1960s. I remember saying to him, "Emil, you don't have any gray hair." He said, "No, Lou. Gotta keep the girls happy. I dye my hair." I said, "Ah, but you have a bald spot on the top. It's kind of brown." And he looked at me and winked and he said, "Shoe polish." He died a couple of years ago (in 2022) at age ninety-five, and I miss him every day, along with many others who miss him.

Once we had our starter hockey league up and running, we expanded it to have about 900 kids. We had a rink in Riverdale, right next to a cookie factory, which wafted out all these delicious cookie smells while kids played hockey. And there was a rink that popped up in Staten Island. We could practice on that rink for two hours every Saturday morning.

There was a rink in Brooklyn's Prospect Park that they let us use for hockey. And then the Abe Stark rink opened on Coney Island.

Hockey was humming and buzzing in New York City. And look at where things stand today. We have kids playing across the New York metropolitan area, as well as in Connecticut, and New Jersey, and we have kids playing in the NHL. And this is how it all started.

How I started as a coach is a funny story. I was helping to run the league by being the guy who put all the teams together and found the coaches. I didn't have any desire or interest to be a coach. It was fun to hang out with everybody, and I was still playing roller hockey, even if I couldn't skate very well. I just loved the hockey culture.

Bart Grillo came to me one night in 1968, and said, "Lou, I need a favor from you." I asked him what was up. "Well, the coach of a midget team can't make it, and I need you to coach them." Midgets are the fifteen- and sixteen-year-olds, so they have been playing for a while. So I said, "Well, I'll try it, but I don't know what to do."

Which was true. I did not know how to coach a hockey team. I decided to go to the library in Canarsie, Brooklyn, to read up on hockey coaching. The only hockey book that they had in that library turned out to be one of the greatest hockey books ever written. It's called *The Hockey Handbook* by Lloyd Percival. I must have read that book thirty times in three months, trying to gain some knowledge and wanting to know more.

Percival had coached hockey in Canada, and had a show, "The Sports College on the Air," which had some 800,000 listeners on CBC Radio. In 1963, Percival opened the Fitness Institute,[1] which was celebrated for its rigorous scientific fitness testing and sports training methods. Percival's book revealed to me that there was a scientific basis behind what hockey players needed to play at the top of their game. I inhaled it.

This is how Percival opens his book:

> Skating is to hockey what throwing is to baseball, what tackling is to football, or what footwork is to tennis. It is the most important fundamental.
>
> Our research has shown that in an average full length game, players skate from two to three miles. When poor line changes are used, players

skate as far as four miles per game. Skating is what the player does most. It is the foundation on which everything else is built.[2]

I mean, he had my full attention from the start, and what he presented was fascinating to me before I even stepped behind a coaching bench. I also didn't want to look like a dope with these kids. I wanted to be able to say something other than "change lines."

As I mentioned, there wasn't even a bench at the rink in Flushing. There was a stairwell, and still, we produced Hall of Famers. So you don't need fancy buildings and rinks. You need coaches and players who want to learn and to work hard to succeed.

So I went "behind the bench," and while I forget what I did in that first game, I know that the kids knew me and they were respectful kids, so they listened to what I had extracted from Lloyd Percival's magnificent book. I made sure everybody played that night, and that was always our goal every night: to make sure every kid played.

Another time, the coach didn't show up, and finally he just quit. His was not a good team, and he didn't want to coach anymore. So I coached that team through the rest of the season in 1969. That's how I got into coaching. Because other coaches didn't show up and I happened to be there.

I also had natural leadership qualities, and I know now that leadership is the most important quality, along with courage, that you need to be the coach of anything. By courage I mean the ability to make a decision and then carry it out, as there will always be a lot of voices telling you what to do. You have to have the courage of your convictions. You also have to listen. I learned that I could do both.

You also need to be organized. I was always voted the captain on any team in several different sports which I played because I was organized. I would get up at five in the morning and prepare our baseball field. I would rake and clean it and make all the lines on the field with flour I stole from my mother. Because if I didn't do it, nobody would do it. My friends and I would play on summer mornings until 9 a.m., which is when the big kids showed up and kicked us off. I resented it and vowed that I would always let anyone who wanted to play whatever sport I was involved in have the chance to play it.

While I loved playing roller hockey, I never had a chance to really play ice hockey. So, like Lloyd Percival told me at the very beginning of his wonderful book, I had to learn to ice skate better. But I had pretty good hands and a pretty good hockey sense, and I knew the game.

I watched New York Rangers games every chance I could get, and I went to most of them. I had season tickets, which cost seventy bucks for the season. I actually had two seats, so it was $140. It worked out to $2 a game per seat for thirty-five home games, and they never made the play-offs until the 1966–67 season and did so each year until the 1974–75 season, so then I had to buy playoff tickets. I was happy to do that.

It was wonderful to be able to watch all these spectacular players from the 1960s in the NHL. And I was in the first row on the balcony, in the corner seat. So it was like a perfect classroom where I was close enough to hear the players talking. I had a good feel for how professional hockey players played because I spent a lot of time watching them.

So all of those things along with Bart Grillo's request to do him a favor combined to get me into coaching and to stick with it. And given my own competitive streak, once I had started, I wanted to get better.

Even with all my practical hockey experience, I knew that I had a lot to learn, and I began the next part of my coaching journey almost by accident. And I began it in the hottest days of the Cold War, when surprisingly, it was our archenemy, the Russians, who were going to show me the way forward.

CHAPTER 4

Back in the USSR

IF YOU WERE BORN IN THE LATE TWENTIETH CENTURY OR AFTER, IT may be hard to imagine the animosity that was shared between the United States and the USSR during the Cold War. I had been in the army in the 1960s, and I was stationed in West Germany, and we knew all about the Russians on the other side of the Berlin Wall, keeping people miserable in East Germany. And keeping them so in many other countries in Eastern Europe.

However, if you were a hockey guy, then the Russians were something majestic to behold, and as soon as I saw them play, I knew that they had a lot to teach me. After all, I started out by teaching myself. I could stand to learn from a country that clearly knew how to play the game I loved.

The year was 1969, and I was twenty-four years old. On Sunday, we'd all go to church in Brooklyn in the morning, and then we'd go to one of my grandmothers' houses for these big Italian Sunday dinners. There would be fifteen to twenty members of my family at the table. We'd have a wonderful meal, and we would sit for three or four hours, telling jokes and stories. But it was a little boring, as you were stuck in the house all the time, so this one dinner in spring I was bored and asked if I could go watch TV in my grandmother's bedroom. She said sure.

So I went in there and turned on the TV, and started turning the dial to find a channel I wanted to watch. Anyone who was conscious at that time will know what the words "The thrill of victory, the agony of defeat" meant. It meant ABC's *Wide World of Sports* was on, and that was great for me because I would watch any sport, anytime. Little did I know how life-changing it would be when the announcer said, "We now take you to Stockholm, Sweden, to watch the gold medal game of the World Championships, International Ice Hockey Federation, between Sweden and the Soviet Union."

And away we went to Stockholm, and I was in awe. I had never seen that kind of hockey before. I had gone to hundreds of New York Rangers games, and I had seen the best that NHL had to offer, but I'd never seen anything like what I was seeing now on this little black-and-white TV, with tin foil on the end of its rabbit ears aerial to improve reception. I was saying to myself, "This is fantastic hockey! Look at these guys skate! Look at their skill in making and receiving passes."

It was very different from the hockey I had seen, which tended to be up and down the rink. These players were using all the space available, going across the rink, and playing a puck possession game, improvising when they had to, like you see on the soccer field. It was fantastic.

The Soviets won the game, but the Swedes were good, too. The camera zoomed in on the Soviet bench, and the announcer said, "That's the Soviet head coach, Anatoly Tarasov." And his name was also written underneath his image on the screen, so I grabbed a pen and wrote it down on a piece of paper. Then I folded up the piece of paper and put it in my pocket.

I was wearing a sport coat because I had gone to church earlier, and we would dress up. But I figured that since I'd been wearing this sport coat four or five times in a row to church, that I had better bring it in to get it dry cleaned or I might be sitting at my own table at these wonderful Sunday dinners.

So, the next day, I went to the cleaners across from where I was living in my own little second-floor apartment on Cropsey Avenue in Brooklyn, not too far from Coney Island. I left the coat to be cleaned. As I was leaving, the woman said, "Sir, sir, I went through the pockets," which they do as a matter of form before cleaning. She had this folded piece of paper in her hand. I asked her what it was, and she said, "I don't know, it looks like some place or someone's name." I told her to just throw it away.

She said, "Oh, please sir, just take it." I took the folded piece of paper, and I remember walking out of the cleaners and across the street to my apartment. I remembered why I had written the name on it: Anatoly Tarasov. So I got a pencil and a piece of paper and started to write a letter to Anatoly Tarasov. I was careful to be neat, and as clear as possible. I complimented him on winning the World Championships, which I never even heard of before that day I saw him on the *Wide World of Sports*. And I told him how much I enjoyed the high skill level of his team, and of his opponent, Sweden. I wrote that I wanted to be able to teach my players, my team of kids, to play better. And I thought he could teach me to do that.

I didn't have a clue where to send it, so I addressed it to "Anatoly Tarasov, Head Coach, USSR national hockey team, Moscow, USSR." Then I folded up my letter and put it in a normal envelope and brought it to the post office. I didn't know how many stamps to put on it, so the guy at the post office looked at it, and saw where it was going, and said, "That will be $3.75."

That's worth $30 today, but back then it was still a shock. I made $60 a week with my job installing air conditioners and I had to pay rent of $75 a month on this beautiful studio apartment I had in Brooklyn, and I had other bills. I didn't have to worry about food—my grandmother and my mother would come to my apartment and put prepared foods and groceries in the fridge and do my laundry—but paying one-seventh or so of my weekly salary to send a letter that would maybe get to a guy in the USSR was an extravagance that I could not afford. So I said, "Thanks, but no thanks."

Then the post office clerk said, "Why don't you rewrite it on Par Avion?" This was an air mail form that was so thin it was like tissue paper, and it was a lot cheaper. And I said, "I have no time to do that. I gotta go to work!" I came that close to missing the opportunity to change my life, but something told me to spend the time and rewrite the letter on the Par Avion form. So I did, and away it went across the world and through the Iron Curtain.

Time passed, maybe a couple of months. I never got mail, just bills. One day, I went to check the mailbox and I saw this letter with strange writing on it. The return address was in Russian Cyrillic writing, and I couldn't read it—I didn't even know what it meant. I even turned the letter upside down to see if it made sense, but it did not. Then I opened it, and the letter was in English. To me. From Anatoly Tarasov.

He had written it on a typewriter, which had run out of black ink ribbon, so the letter was a kind of rainbow, in black, then red, then green, then blue. I liked that he had done that and wasn't ashamed to mail it. I found out why later. He said, "Well, the girl at the Red Army office knows some English. And she kept running out of ribbons. Lou, we didn't have a lot of money. We didn't have a lot of materials. Like you capitalists." It wasn't a professional letter, and the English wasn't perfect, but Anatoly Tarasov's sly wit shone through from the very first sentence.

He said, "First, I want to thank you so very much for writing and for complimenting my team, for winning the championship. But we Russians know that in hockey, when Canadians compliment you in hockey, they're stealing from you. They want you to go easy the next time." That was his attitude. And I remember the first time I met him, he would elaborate on this theme, and as you will see, he liked my answer.

It had not been easy to get to Moscow to meet with Tarasov. I borrowed $350 from my friend Walter Yaciuk for my travel expenses, and I had no idea what I was in for or what I was doing. Tarasov told me to get a visa and let him know when I was coming. If you called the Soviet Union embassy in those days, it would take a week to make an appointment at a specific time even to just speak to somebody. It was very complicated. Yet I was so naive as not to be nervous about it at all.

I flew over to Moscow, and it was a dreary Sunday in 1970 when I landed. It was raining and my memory of it to this day is that looking out on the city was like looking at a black-and-white movie from the 1920s.

At the Moscow airport, everything was strange. I couldn't read the Cyrillic signs, so I just followed other people to the baggage claim. I noticed everybody looked the same, and that nobody was smiling at anyone, anywhere. Even when I went through customs, I tried to smile and make small talk in English, because I certainly didn't know Russian. And these customs guys in their military uniforms with red stars on their hats just stared at me, then stamped my passport. It wasn't a warm welcome. At the baggage carousel I saw a guy holding a sign with my name on it in English. I went over and he couldn't speak English either, but he drove me to see Tarasov.

It was very dark and dank as we drove along. Everybody was dressed in gray and black. There was no color. There were no restaurants that I could see, and there were no shops open. And this is Moscow, one of the premier cities of the world and certainly the greatest in the USSR, and it was very desolate.

However, having said that, once I got to know the place, the people were fine. I can judge people pretty well, coming as I do from New York City. That's one of the best qualities I have. I can read people and I will know if they're phony. And the feeling I got from the Russians was that they were genuine. They were just decent people. They didn't want to hurt me. They just didn't have much to offer. But if you got a smile from them, it meant something.

So I finally met Anatoly Tarasov, and he was wearing his military uniform, and he wasn't smiling. He was an officer in the Red Army. In 1946, Tarasov was a twenty-six-year-old Central Soviet Army player-coach. At the time, Russia had no ice hockey tradition, although bandy, which is kind of like hockey played with a ball, was an established sport. Tarasov received an order from the communist government's Committee on Physical Education and Sports to prepare a team in what it deemed "Canadian hockey" so the USSR could compete on the international stage.

Tarasov later admitted that in the early days, he had no idea whether he was on the right track when he started organizing the squad. They could skate, and he built on that. He told me that they "became great skaters because when you're skating every day, on a rink the size of the soccer field, you'll become a pretty good skater pretty fast. And you want to stay warm because winter is very brutal, so you want to keep moving."

So while the team could skate, they lacked proper training tools—no hockey gloves and only crude equipment. For coaching guidance, Tarasov toted around a tattered pamphlet, explaining the rules of ice hockey.

What he also had, as a tutor, was Soviet-occupied Czechoslovakia, and the Czechs played a very fine game of hockey. It was a game that they had learned from a Canadian, Mike Buckna. The irony is that Tarasov's hockey orders to marshal a team to play like Canadians actually learned from a team that played an old style of Canadian hockey.

On a November morning in 1935, Mike Buckna found himself a long way from Trail, British Columbia, where he had starred for the Smoke Eaters, the smelter town's legendary hockey team, or rather, teams, as the "Smokies" have existed as both junior and senior teams since the 1920s. Now he was standing in the homeland of his parents, who had immigrated to Canada in 1898 to open a small hotel in Trail. While the landscape might have been unfamiliar, Buckna certainly knew all about the building in front of him here in Prague: it was an ice rink.

The Czechs didn't know it at first, that this twenty-two-year-old Canadian, clutching a newspaper clipping about tryouts for the national team, would be the savior of hockey in their country, but player-coach Jiri Trzicka knew that if he didn't figure something out fast, Buckna and his friend were going to be gone, on their way to Slovakia later that morning. So he frantically phoned the team's manager at home. "I was given a strict order, 'Try them and if they are good enough call me!'" Trzicka would later tell the Trail Historical Society. "I lent him skates, stick and puck. I was by myself, an examining as well as a hiring committee."

Buckna skated around on the uneven ice surface, and it was soon apparent to everyone that he wasn't going to be leaving for Slovakia that day. "His skating and his moves were inimitable with lighting speed," recalled Trzicka, "and you could see how happy he was doing it and with such a great enjoyment he did it . . . and that was how we finally got a Canadian player and a coach whom we all well understood and especially he understood us. We had an urge to learn again because Matej [Buckna] was on fire and totally lived for hockey." The Czechs had found their hockey savior by accident.

Buckna taught them how to forecheck, how to rush the puck, and how to take a man right out of the play "instead of giving him just a little push." He taught them conditioning, how to move the puck around with precision, how to break out of their own zone with speed, and how to get rid of the puck fast, to take goalies by surprise. "Basically, I taught them the kind of hockey we were playing in Trail," he said.

He also taught the Czechs a fundamental truth that all the best teams know instinctively: the game is so fluid and fast that fortune's wheel can spin from despair to triumph with one inspired rush. "That's the beauty of hockey," Buckna said. "It's possible to reverse the trend of a game as long as you don't give up."

In March 1939, Nazi Germany was marching on Prague, and Buckna knew that it was time to go back home, with his new wife, Lola Frolikova, whom he married the year before. Buckna would not return to Prague until 1946. The following year, he would coach the Czech national team to its first victory in the World Championships.[1]

In the same year, 1946, Tarasov got his orders to make Soviet hockey into Canadian hockey, and the great Tarasov, with his stocky frame and hangdog face and booming voice, and his love of Bolshoi ballet and grandmaster chess, went to work. He studied, then tinkered, and he borrowed from wherever he could, and he borrowed a lot from the Czechs. And then he stirred the pot with his own substantial hockey genius.

It worked. In 1953, the Soviets won their first International Ice Hockey Federation (IIHF) World Championship. Three years later, they won their first Olympic gold medal, outscoring their opponents 40–9 in seven games. Starting with the 1963 IIHF World Championships, Tarasov's team with the CCCP (USSR) crest—largely composed of his Red Army Moscow players—swept every championship for the next ten years, reaching a pinnacle with the 1972 Olympic gold medal.

By the time I met him, he was a giant of the game. He sat at his desk, scowling at me, and offered me some cookies and tea. He had an interpreter, and through him, asked me, "How old are you?" I was twenty-five. He was fifty-one, or fifty-two. Twice my age. He said, "You know, nobody's ever asked me about how I coach hockey. No Canadians have ever said to me, how do you do this? Or why do you do that? And I adore Bobby Hall. Maurice Richard. I adore them." And then he paused and said, "So you came to steal from me?"

"Yes," I said. What else am I going to say?

"To learn? To learn and steal?"

"Yes."

"Who sent you?" he asked.

"Nobody," I told him. "I want to learn about how you teach your team to transition so well, I want to learn how you create. And your defense is different than in the NHL, too. I coach kids. And I never thought of being a coach. But if I'm going to be a coach, I want to be a good coach. I want to make a difference."

His face lit up with a smile when I said that. He liked what I had said a lot, and then he said to me, "Let me give you advice. At one point I wanted to go to Canada to study the Canadians. I went to the head of the Institute of Physical Sport and Culture in Moscow where I was learning coaching theories and my instructor said to me, 'Anatoly, I'll approve. But why do you want to go to Canada and copy? Why not stay here, save the money? Stay here and come up with something of your own. We have a unique society. Develop a style of hockey unique to Soviets. We played bandy, soccer, and football. We have an idea of tactics. Let's develop all the skills and see what we can do.'"

Tarasov told me that he had done all that. And then he looked me deep in the eye and said, "You can borrow from other schools of hockey but don't copy. I mean, I can't stop you from copying, but don't. You can steal some ideas, some principles. But don't copy and I'll tell you why. There's only one Mona Lisa. Everything else is a copy. And none of them are as good as the original. If you want to be able to compete with the Soviet Union someday, you cannot copy."

I told him I understood, but he wasn't finished. He wanted to make sure I was there for the right reasons. He said, "As a coach, you'll lose prestige if you steal, and players will know you took it from another coach. I get ideas from Canada, Sweden, Czechs [Czechoslovakia at the time], other coaches in the Soviet Union, but I change it a little bit to fit my needs. And I don't want the players to think that I had to steal from somebody else because I wasn't wise enough to come up with something of my own."

He told me that I could help hockey in my country, eventually, because in all his years of coaching, nobody had asked him the question that I had asked: "What are your secrets?"

And he said, "Lou, there are no secrets. Remember this old Russian saying, 'Today's secret is tomorrow's common knowledge.'"

I told him that I had never played ice hockey, but I liked the rough and tumble of it, and to be honest, I liked the fighting. I wondered what his reaction would be to that revelation. He said, "We have boxers to do that. We box. That's what that fighting sport is called. Boxing. Hockey is not fighting. Hockey is a technical game of beauty. And you do need courage and toughness to play it. But it doesn't give you a right to try to intimidate people."

He said, "You Canadians." He always called me a Canadian. "You think you're so tough? Because you fight in hockey. Let me remind you. We're just a little bit tougher. We lost 35 million people, soldiers, and patriots fighting the Nazis. In the Great Patriotic War. We don't have to prove our toughness in sport with fisticuffs. We want to do it with elegance, teamwork, and beauty. We want to make the sport beautiful. But you got to be tough just to play and make it beautiful." And to this day, it's had that kind of an influence on me because it made sense.

I didn't tell him at the time that they lost 35 million people because Stalin killed 30 million of them, but I would tell Tarasov a few things that would get him angry, and he would slam his first on the table, and his interpreter would look frightened. But gradually, we came to understand each other, me, a twenty-five-year-old Brooklyn guy, and this colonel in the Red Army who was convinced that I was a Canadian there to steal from him, and who actually liked that fact.

The Russians hosted me to the best of their circumstances. I lived in a room in the barracks in the Training Center. It was a basic room, with a single bed, and a little bathroom where the shower was a hose that came out of the bathroom ceiling. They gave me a big block of brown soap that must have weighed three pounds. You couldn't hold it in your hand as you washed—it was too big and heavy. So I would wet my hands on that big square of perfumeless soap and step into the shower.

Or rather, step under the shower. I would take a shower standing in front of the toilet bowl and the water would go everywhere. It eventually emptied down into the drain in the center of the bathroom floor, and then I would use the one towel they had given me to wipe everything clean and dry myself.

We'd have breakfast every morning at the Training Center. It was healthy food. I liked the fruits, some of them cooked, and the juices. They had bacon, and different meats. They would eat salad at breakfast. For lunch they had little sausages and vegetables. They had potato pancakes with sour cream. The soups were delicious. They had specialties like pelmeni, which are like little round pieces of ravioli, which I liked. They had cabbage, sauerkraut, kielbasa, and different salamis. A good mix of protein and vegetables and carbohydrates.

I never dined outside of the Training Center. I don't even know if Moscow had restaurants in those days. The big wide avenues were empty. Moscow is a beautiful city, and even so when I was first there. There were chandeliers in the subways and art on the walls. I came to like the country, and the people.

The hockey was something else. Players sharpened their own skates on a machine that looked like something in Uncle Charlie's garage that he sharpened screwdrivers on. All the players carried their own equipment and bags. I was in one dressing room that had a dirt floor with rubber mats over it.

In one of the other dressing rooms there was a pipe coming out of the ceiling with ice cold water in it, and the players showered there, and no one complained. They would wash their jerseys by hand in the basins, and then hang them up to dry.

I got to go on the ice for practice, and I even scored a goal on a big eighteen-year-old goalie, named Vladislav Tretiak. I had the puck and skated in on him and said, in English, "Get ready" and then I backhanded the puck over his shoulder. He was very annoyed by that, and the next time I got close to his net, he charged out at me like some big terrifying beast. We would become friends, but that's how we began.

With Anatoly Tarasov everything was business, but he had fun while he was doing it, and he was a champion. He was a showman, like the maestro of a three-ring circus at practice. He had players in every zone, doing unbelievable things. And he was an effective motivator. He was dramatic. I didn't understand Russian, but I understood a little when he would speak to his players because he was so full of drama and so expressive. I saw their reactions and could figure it out.

I think the best way to describe Tarasov's philosophy is that he was much more of a romantic than he was practical. And there was nothing wrong with his practical approach. He told me something very practical one time that helped me then, and that I hope has helped countless players. He asked me a pointed question. "What do you do when you have a great offensive player who loves the attack? And is very good at it. Do you take him?"

He paused and looked at me, then continued. "It's my belief that Canadians coaches—" and I would again say that I was not a Canadian, but an American, and he would wave his hand dismissively and say, "That is even worse."

Then he continued, "Let's say Canadian coaches have a very good offensive player, and who loves to play the attacking game. And they want to make him better defensively. And they'll spend a lot of time trying to make this player who has innate talents, and a strong desire to attack, into a better defensive player. We even have a few coaches like that in the Soviet Union. I understand their point. But, Lou, you should think of it like this, at least think of it. If I'm going to build a house, I want the best person, a specialist and foundations person to start building my house. And when he's done, I want to bring in the best men I can find: the best plumber, electrician, the best carpenter and so on. I want to bring in experts, specialists in their field, because I want a strong, strong house."

He paused and looked at me, to make sure I understood. Then he continued, "I don't want a general handyman to build my home. Why would you want a general handyman type player to build your team? I have players who are great on the attack, and I have great defensemen. So do you want to build a team of highly skilled specialists or a team of general handymen?" And I never ever would have even thought of that. But he changed my hockey team thinking forever.

I remember, pretty much, every single word this man ever said. I can hear his deep booming voice in my head. I knew him very well and would come to spend months with him over a period of more than twenty years. But it could have all ended on that first visit to him, when I said to Tarasov, "Okay, here's what I need. Can you give me six drills? For defense, and for the offense?"

He pounded his fist on the desk. And he was wearing his colonel's uniform for the Red Army. And he was intimidating. The interpreter was petrified. Tarasov said to me, "I'll give you the six drills you want, but you have to bring me one hundred of yours tomorrow at 6 a.m."

I tried to speak but he banged his hand on the desk again and yelled in my face. "So what did he say?" I asked the interpreter, who told me that he said to stay silent. And then they showed me to my little room. I sat in that room with a single light bulb over my very basic desk and a wooden chair. They gave me a red pencil and a regular pencil and some paper on which to diagram my one hundred drills for Anatoly Tarasov.

I stayed up the whole night, and I could think of only forty drills. I was making stuff up. I finally said to myself, "I don't care if he throws me out. I'm ready to go home. This is exhausting."

When I showed up at his office at 6 a.m. he was in a better mood than the one in which I had left him. He showed some hospitality. There was a young woman in his office, wearing a white apron and a chef's hat, and she had a food wagon. She served me and Tarasov and the interpreter some tea with honey, and fruit juice and some little cakes and breads and sunny-side up eggs. It was very nice.

Then Tarasov said, "Okay, now let's get to work. Show me your exercises." He called drills "exercises." I showed him my stack of drills, and he looked at the first one very carefully, and asked me questions, looking over his glasses on the tip of his nose with his bushy eyebrows arched. He said, "Well, what position is in this play? You don't know how to do the symbols properly. The defenseman should be a triangle, and the forward should be a circle." He was detailed to the nth degree.

Then he took a red pencil and put a big X through my drill and said "*Nyet!*" and tossed it on the floor. He said, "You didn't give me the hundred exercises I asked for." I said, "The sixty that I didn't do would be worse than the forty I did."

He liked that. He even grinned a little bit. I asked him if I could see his exercises. And he said "*kanyashna*" which means "of course." I had learned the word. Then he showed me the first one, which was so elaborate. I had never seen so many triangles and circles and lines, which were curved, like little parentheses. It was wild.

When I finished looking at his exercise, I made up questions because I didn't want to look like I was dumb. I asked him questions that made no sense, but he answered anyway. And I was saying to myself, "This guy is just going to destroy me. Screw him and get on a plane tonight and go home."

I was really exhausted and felt beaten up, because he was hammering me with this stuff. And I looked at his exercise and I took his red pencil from him, and I put an X through it, and I said *"Nyet!"* and then I threw it on the floor the way he had done to mine. And the interpreter was staring in shock at me. "Mister Vairo, you drop ice rink diagram on the floor?"

I said, "No, I didn't drop it on the floor. I threw it on the floor."

Tarasov had a quizzical look on his face, sort of like when you talk to your pet dog and they turn their head and they look at you as if to say, "What are you telling me?" He had that look, and he stood up.

I could see that the interpreter was extremely nervous. Tarasov said "Lou!" and turned to sign language. He gestured for me to stand up, so I stood up. I didn't know what was going to happen. Was he going to take a swing at me? Pull out his pistol and shoot me? Instead, he put his arms out and gave me a big hug. I saw the interpreter relax—just a little bit.

Tarasov said, "Lou. Do you realize there is not a single coach in all of the Soviet Union who would ever put a red marker on Anatoly Tarasov's work and throw it to the floor? Not a single coach. You have very little experience, but you have something much more important if you're going to be a coach. You have courage. You have to know the climate between our countries is tense," which I certainly did know. "And here you are, alone, on a visa, at my invitation in Moscow, our capital city of the Soviet Union, speaking to a colonel in the Red Army, and a famous hockey coach—worldwide and not just in my country—and you're ready to fight with me? Nobody in the Soviet Union, *nobody* would do what you just did. Not because they're more polite than you, but because they lack the courage that you have. You have the first most important ingredient to be a coach, you have courage. It's a very difficult job, and responsibility. And you'll have to make decisions. Training players and coaching them in games, where sometimes taking risks is the proper strategy to improve the player to win a game. And you have this basic fundamental ability. The rest you can learn."

I always told him the truth. And he loved it. From that day on, we were really friends.

And I was very happy that I was in Moscow, learning from Tarasov, who would teach me much over the more than twenty years of our great friendship, one born because I turned the channel on an old TV on a bored Sunday afternoon back in 1969. And with that turn of the dial, it changed the way I would teach hockey, which would change the American game, and my life, for the better.

CHAPTER 5

The First Championship

WHEN I ANNOUNCED MY PLANS TO GO TO MOSCOW TO LEARN SOME more about ice hockey from a Russian master, my family thought I was insane to go to that godless Communist nation. And they were all very relieved that I made it back alive and well. Propaganda against the Soviet Union in America was strong at the height of the Cold War. Consider what the *New York Times* was reporting in June 1970 under the headline "Chilly Breeze from Moscow":

> Moscow's three top leaders have underscored this week the chasm that separates the two superpowers, the United States and the Soviet Union. Thus Communist party chief Brezhnev has emphasized that Soviet-American differences "are really deep"; President Podgorny characterized relations as "in a kind of frozen state," and Premier Kosygin attacked this country as the "main source of international tension." To these unfriendly words, Moscow has now added an announcement that it is sending additional aid to North Vietnam.[1]

So the USSR was seen as this communist villain that wanted to end our way of life, and I supposed that is what my family expected me to say when I returned. However, what I told them was that my trip to Moscow was better than any college education I could have received on the subjects of hockey and life. I went right into the heart of the so-called enemy, and what did I see?

People who were as interested in me as I was in them. They asked me a lot of questions. I found them to be well-educated. I found the USSR to be a "third world" country, from what I had read and heard about "third world" countries. I didn't see any cars other than government vehicles, but there were plenty of buses, both electric and gas, and they had trolley cars. I told my family it was no different than in Brooklyn about twenty years earlier. I said some of the people were a little standoffish because they get similar propaganda from their government about Americans. There wasn't a lot of smiling, but then, they didn't smile at each other. But in general, the people were kind. They were very nice to me.

My grandmother always said that there was good and bad in every culture, and I had seen that to be true in my own. And you shouldn't judge everybody by the flag which flies over them. She was a wise woman. I explained that all the Russians wanted, to my eyes, was to be able to make a living and put some food on the table. They wanted a safe roof over their heads, and those that had good political connections had another roof, a summer house called a *dacha*. It was the dream of every Soviet citizen, to go to the countryside in the summertime, to the beach, on the Black Sea. Just like Americans with money went to Cape Cod, or Martha's Vineyard, and those without went to Coney Island. And like us, the Russians loved their sports. They supported their athletes, and they were proud of their country like most Americans are proud of their county.

So I had all this new hockey knowledge bouncing around in my head, and pretty soon I would get a chance to use it. I was a volunteer coach in the New York Metropolitan league that Emil Francis had started and I coached the peewee team. And I was working my day job, installing air conditioners for Bart Grillo.

One day I got a call from the father of a player I had coached. Bobby Crawford played for me when he was little, a squirt and a peewee, and he was a good right winger who would go on to play with Colorado and Detroit in the NHL. Bobby was playing for a team in Minnesota called the Austin Mavericks in the Midwest Junior Hockey League, who had just finished their first season.

The Mavericks were started by two excellent hockey men, Walter Bush, who was president of the Minnesota North Stars, and Murray Williamson, whom Tarasov loved. Murray was originally from Winnipeg, and he coached at the University of Minnesota, and he coached the 1972 US Olympic hockey team to a silver medal in Sapporo, Japan. And along with another Canadian guy, Andre Beaulieu, they formed a junior league, the first real junior league at a high level in the United States. One of the franchises was in Austin, and the others were in St. Paul, Fargo, St. Cloud, and Minneapolis.

Bobby's father told me that the Mavericks had lost their coach, Leon Abbott. I knew who Leon was. He had coached at Boston University, and then he became a player agent. And he was making a lot of money as an agent, but he had also been well paid in Austin. They paid him $40,000 to coach that team in 1974.

And the Austin Mavericks had finished dead last. Leon had gone to greener pastures, so to speak, and they were looking for a coach. "Bobby loved it when he played for you," his father said. "He asked me to see if I could find Lou and find out if he would be interested in coming out here to coach. Bobby would love to play for you again. Do you have any interest?"

I didn't know. I had a job. I had my own apartment. I was already coaching two teams in the New York City League. So I told him the truth. "I don't know."

"How much are you making?" he asked. I told him the truth about that, too. Because I was working off the books, I made $60 a week. He asked if I could live on that.

"I am living on it," I told him. "My rent takes most of it. I have a car. It's free. It was given to me by Bart Grillo, who I work for in air conditioning."

He told me that I should give it some thought. I was a little bit annoyed that he called me because I liked the way my life was. I didn't want to go to Austin, Minnesota. Yet even so, I was intrigued by the call.

The next day I got another call from a guy named Lynn McAllister, who introduced himself as the general manager of the Austin Mavericks. Lynn told me that they had an opening for a coaching position and echoed Bobby's father in saying again that the reason that he was calling me was that one of their better players told them that he played for me in New York, and that they should try to get me to come out to Austin to coach.

He asked if I would be interested in the job, and I told him that I had a pretty good life in Brooklyn. I asked him to tell me about the league. He said that it was a good league, with many good players. "Here's the deal," he continued. "We have a training camp coming up in a couple of weeks." It was now June. "You come out and run that camp and pick a team. And the terms are pretty good. We would pay $40,000 a year for you to coach, and we pay for your telephone bill, and we'll provide you with a vehicle. Do you have any interest?"

He also said that he needed a recommendation other than from Bobby Crawford. So I called Emil Francis and explained the whole thing to him. He was very kind to me. He asked how much they offered to pay me. I told him $40,000. I'll never forget what he said. He said, "I'll take the job myself." And at the time, he was the GM, coach, and vice president of the New York Rangers. He asked for the name and number of the guy in Austin and said he would call him and sing my praises.

Then I called another friend, another great hockey man. Fred Shero was coaching the Philadelphia Flyers and I told Fred what was up, and he said, "Oh, geez, you gotta do it, Lou. You gotta take that. That'll be right up your alley. You got to go."

So I gave Fred the number for Lynn McCallister, and he said he would call him. Later that night I got a call from Lynn McAllister, who was a hockey fan, and who knew who Emil Francis and Fred Shero were. "I couldn't believe it," he said. "And they both highly recommended you. That's all I need to know. Okay, next you'll hear from the team president, Jim Weber."

The next day, I got a call from Jim Weber, and he introduced himself. And he said, "Lou, I understand Lynn, our GM, called you and you guys had a discussion. What did Lynn promise you?"

I told him, and he said that there was going to be a change in that offer. He said, "We can't do anything like that. We lost our shirts last year—$70,000. We're eight local businessmen in a small town here in

Minnesota with a population of 25,000, and we wanted to bring hockey to southern Minnesota, where it's not very popular. We're in football and basketball country, but we thought we'd do something nice. And we're just all individuals chipping in and trying to get done. But we took a good beating. We need to take a bank loan out now to cover our expenses. Our families are not very happy with us, but we want to make it work. You can use my office to make any business calls, or any calls you need to make. I'll find you a used car. We'll figure it out."

So I said, "What *are* you offering me?"

He told me that they were not offering the job, yet. They wanted to meet me first and see me in action. He told me that they had a tryout camp in Golden Valley, Minnesota, coming up in about three weeks, and that they would fly me out to Rochester, Minnesota, and he would pick me up at the airport.

And then he added a strong dose of reality. He said, "As far as the salary goes, we'll pay you $2,000 a year and we won't provide you a phone, or an apartment, or a car."

I called Emil Francis and told him the story had changed and told him how. I told him that I didn't know what to do. The salary is $2,000. And there was no car, and no phone. And he said to me, "You want to coach, so don't judge it until you have seen it. Get out of New York City. There are limits here and they have pretty good hockey players in that Minnesota area." He said that they were going to be producing NHL players. I could accomplish a lot there.

So I flew to Minnesota and Jim Weber met me at the airport. He was a wild military guy, who was a former police officer who now ran his own insurance adjusting business. And Jim told me that I was going to stay at his house, with his wife and four kids. I did, and they were a lovely family.

We went to the training camp in Golden Valley. I met everybody, and I liked them all. Everybody was nice. But I didn't like Minnesota. I missed home. I missed my friends. I said to myself, I'm not going to do this. I'm just not.

I went on the ice, and we were going to start the camp. But then Lynn came on the ice and then another guy came on the ice. I had gathered all the players together and I was introducing myself and getting ready to start. And Lynn and this other guy were interfering, and they shouldn't be doing that. I mean, I had already almost talked myself out of this job whose salary had plummeted from $40,000 to $2,000. However, I was intrigued with the prospect, but now I had this management interference. I could not deal with that, so I had to find out if it was something that would be with me should I take the job.

I blew the whistle and brought everybody in close. I said, "Lynn, I'm going to have to ask you guys to leave the ice. I don't mean to be disrespectful to you, but you're in the way on the ice. If I'm going to do this, I have to do it my way, or I'm not going to do it. Go sit in the stands and evaluate the players from there. You're interfering with what I want to do." Had I made a mistake? Were they going to kick me out of town? I remembered Tarasov told me if you make a mistake, make sure it's your mistake. They didn't like being asked to leave, but they got off the ice. And I stayed on it.

I ran the camp my way. Apparently, my way did not suit everyone, as three players quit. They said "we don't want to play for this guy. He's from Brooklyn, he hasn't even played ice hockey."

Jim Weber said to me and Lynn, "They're pretty good players. But they don't want to be here."

I had heard enough, so I replied, "If you want me to be your coach, and they don't want to be here, I'm not going to try to talk them into being here. Make them free agents. Let them go where they think they'll be happy. You know, guys, you finished in last place with them, you can finish in last place without them. It's not like they led you to the championship. Let them go."

They had some good players on that team. They were smaller, but they could skate, and they could play. And they were nice kids too. So we negotiated a deal on a Saturday night, and I accepted $2,000 a year until the end of the season in April.

When I got back to Brooklyn, I called Emil Francis and told him that I had gone to Minnesota and had run the training camp and had accepted the job. Emil was pleased. And then he said something to me that I loved to hear. "You can eat a bologna sandwich as well as an eight-ounce tenderloin and you get used to the bologna, Lou. This is your hockey college. You're going to school in a highly respected area of hockey in America. Pros are coming out of there and they're going to keep coming. I think it's a very good move for you if you want to have a career in the game. And if you want to coach, you have to coach at the highest level possible each step of the way." And at the end of our call, he said one more thing to me that I really appreciated. "Lou, if you run into any trouble financially, you got my phone number, give me a call. I'll help you out."

So I went to Minnesota. I started summer training off ice right away, in July. And the players were pissed off at me, but they came to camp. It was wicked training, most of it dryland, like I had seen Tarasov do. At first the players didn't like the idea of this heavy-duty physical training, but they got into it. And the players could tell that they were getting quicker and stronger, more agile, and I could see a camaraderie was developing among them.

I said to Jim Weber that we had to do this season right or we would finish in last place again, and so I told him how that would happen based on what Fred Shero once told me. I had asked Fred if he were giving a young guy like me advice, what would it be? And Fred Shero, coach of the Stanley Cup–winning Flyers, said, "It would be ham and eggs." I asked him what he meant. He said, "We have a chicken and a pig. If you want to make it in this sport or any other thing in life, you have to be committed. It's not enough to be dedicated. The chicken is dedicated, and it lays an egg every day. But the pig is committed."

I instilled it into my players that they had to be committed. We had a training camp on the ice for two days, then one day off ice training. We didn't even have twenty players, but we picked up a few cuts from other teams. I was teaching them that hybrid style of hockey off ice combined with on ice training. There was a big Anatoly Tarasov influence at work out there. And little by little, the players came to love it, because they were in the best shape of their young lives.

We played our first game of the season up in St. Paul, to a pretty good crowd and a lot of college scouts. And the St. Paul coach was Doug Woog, who had replaced Herb Brooks, who had gone to coach at the

University of Minnesota. I didn't know Herb Brooks at the time, but I would come to know him pretty soon.

We were confident going into our first game, and it was horrible. St. Paul had a big, tough, strong team, and they were good. And yet, we did some things in that game that were also good. And the final score was 12–6 for the other guys. I was devastated.

I never spoke on the team bus to anybody as we rode home. Next day, I was sitting in a chair in the house we were renting and where we were letting some of the players live until they could get billeted. I lived there too, and cooked all their meals for $1 a day for them.

And as I was sitting there, one of the players, Mitch Corbin, came in. This was a Sunday morning, and Mitch was always chipper no matter what time of day, and he said, "Hey, Coach," and he sat down. He saw that I was glum, and he asked me what was wrong. "You're always full of enthusiasm!" he said.

I told him that I was disappointed in myself after our loss the night before, and that I just hoped I hadn't destroyed the players on the team. "I know you all want to get scholarships and go to college or play in a higher league next year," I said. I told him that the game the night before was a disaster and that I felt terrible because I was responsible.

He said, "What!!? We were great. Maybe if Fedoruk would have played a little better in goal, we could have won that game."

And I said, "No, we got hammered. I feel embarrassed for all of you guys. And I put you through this."

He shook his head and said, "Come on, Coach! I'm not buying that. We'll show you we can play. I love what you're doing. We can play. So don't be like that and blame yourself. I never want to see that again."

That's what this wise and sane kid said to me. He gave me a pep talk. And we're still friends. He sends me a Christmas card every year.

I thought about what he had said, and it started to get my blood boiling again, and to raise the temperature on my natural competitiveness. And I knew Mitch was right. Our next game was an away game, and we dominated that team at home. We beat them eight to nothing. They hardly ever had the puck. We embarrassed them. And we won five more games in a row after that victory.

I was on my own roll in Austin as well. I had a few side hustles going to top up my lowly salary. I moved out of the rented house for the players once we got them all billeted and into a lakeside cottage, which was about six hundred square feet in total. I also started painting houses. It was winter so I was painting interiors of houses, and it was horrible. I had to use oil paint and clean the brushes with turpentine in the days before latex paint. Just like I had done in the army.

I also taught an Italian cooking class two nights a week at the local high school. And three days a week I worked at the Village Pump washing pots and pans at lunch hour. I worked for three hours a day and I think I made $15 each day. So I managed. I bought a car for $100 and drove it in a town of 20,000 people that only had one traffic light. It wouldn't start one morning in December, and it never started again.

But the Austin Mavericks could not stop. After our first six straight wins, we followed that with five more wins in a row. And we won the league with twenty-eight wins in fifty games. We won the national championship that year against established clubs. We had made the Austin Mavericks into a championship team. Rather, I had given them the plan, and they had played their hearts out to win it all.

As for those three kids who quit before we got started, well, I've run into all three of them over the years. The son of one of them ended up playing in the NHL, and he even ended up playing for me for a few games. His father said that leaving the Austin team in my first year behind the bench was the worst decision of his life, one he would take to his grave. He said he had no idea that we could accomplish what we did. And I thought the same on one Sunday at the start of the season. Mitch Corbin saved my so-called career at that dark moment when he gave me his pep talk.

But it was my trip to the USSR to learn from Anatoly Tarasov that fueled my career. I had taken what I had learned from him and not only put it into practice in the United States but had shown that it could work. A team that had finished in last place had, thanks to this hybrid method of training, finished top of the league as champions. And now, my work in Austin had been noticed by people higher up the hockey food chain. Soon, I would be on my way up the chain, too.

CHAPTER 6

The Godfather

I STAYED COACHING IN AUSTIN, MINNESOTA, BUILDING ON THE SUCCESS that we were having in playing a very different brand of hockey. It didn't matter who we played, as we kept on winning. I saw how the players loved to play this style of creative, puck possession hockey. And they loved the training for it, once they got into it. And I was having a good time, too. I was learning how to be a coach by winning hockey games.

And I also learned how to deal with injuries. We had a great goalie, Tom Hazensahl. There was nobody close to his talent. He would have been an NHL goalie of the highest order if he had not lost an edge by catching his skate on a little ridge in the ice in a game against the St. Paul Vulcans. He went down and twisted his knee. He had to have surgery. He came back eventually, but he never regained his form.

We would have won the league again, but Tom only played twelve games before he was lost for the season, and we finished in second place, with the same number of wins as Bloomington Junior Stars, the champions, but one point less than them as they had earned a point for a tie, and we had not. We had one more loss. Those are the margins in sport, and I know that if we had been able to keep Tom healthy, we would have snagged that championship title again.

When I was inducted into the US Hockey Hall of Fame, Tom surprised me. He came up from Virginia, where he's retired and lives now. He told me that those games of that season were the greatest twelve games of his life. He had two shutouts in those twelve games as well.

I was coaching in Austin, and the Mayo Clinic is close, just 30 miles away in Rochester, Minnesota. Bob Fleming and Ken Johanssen, two former Canadians, had come down and played college hockey in the States. They ended up running the Mayo Clinic administratively. The two of them developed a lot of players in Rochester, Minnesota, for their senior team, the Mustangs, who played in the old USHL [US Hockey League] senior league. Other Canadians came and played and ended up living in Rochester, and they developed a fantastic youth hockey program in southern Minnesota. And they loved hockey, of course.

When I was coaching, Fleming and Johansson had heard that this guy from Brooklyn had his team playing a very interesting brand of hockey. Word had spread. And they used to come to games, and they introduced themselves to me and they couldn't have been nicer. One night, at the end of my third season, Bob Fleming called me from the Mayo Clinic. And he said, "Lou, can I meet with you? What's a good night we can meet when you don't have practice or a game or anything?" I told him Thursday night was good, and he asked if we could meet at the Rochester airport.

I had upgraded from my car that had stopped running to a pretty beat-up car that stopped every 10 miles or so, and I would have to put brake fluid in it. I carried a screwdriver in my car, just to handle whatever repairs came up along the way. It's how things had been back in Brooklyn, so I was used to it. I told him it would take me about an hour to get there, and he said that it was only a 30-mile drive. I said, "Well, when you see my car, you will know why it took me longer."

Here I was driving through cornfields, and I was as nervous as I could be. I had two bucks in my pocket, but I had enough gas to make it to the airport and to make it back. I arrived at the airport and went to the restaurant where we were supposed to meet. Little did I know that it was a very nice restaurant, and very expensive.

Bob was there and he greeted me like an old friend. He told me that I was actually there for a "kind of interview" to possibly come work for USA Hockey, which was then known by the acronym AHAUS, which stood for the Amateur Hockey Association of the United States. I hated the acronym. People used to ask me "Is that the American Hospital Association?"

So I was sitting with Bob, and I was a nervous wreck, because I looked at the menu and my eyes popped. This was 1978, and on the menu the most expensive thing was a filet mignon, which cost $12 then, and would cost, with inflation, around $57.35 today.[1] For that princely sum you would get the steak, a baked potato, a vegetable side, and the salad bar. I had $2 to my name, and I didn't know if I had to pay for my own dinner or not, but I knew I could not afford filet mignon.

Bob could, and so he ordered the six-ounce filet and baked potato and asked me what I was going to have. I said, "Well, how about I just have a little dinner salad?" I think the cost of that was $2.50, so even then I was short of funds. I didn't want to appear to be a fool, either, so I was in a jam. I couldn't just drink iced tea, which I could afford, while Bob ate his steak.

Bob knew what I made in Austin, and he could read the look of panic on my face, and he said, "Lou! It's my treat. The Amateur Hockey Association is paying for this."

I was very happy to hear that, so I said, "All right. I'll have the same as you're having, Mr. Fleming." I didn't get to eat steak often, especially filet mignon on my $2,000 a year coaching salary, even with my side hustles. But as Emil Francis had told me, I was at hockey college in Minnesota, so I had to live like a student.

We had a nice dinner and a nice interview, which was more like a conversation than twenty questions. He told me about the personnel they had, and it sounded pretty spare. They had an executive director, a secretary, and a marketing guy. He told me that they would like to bring me on board, but they did not have much of a national coaching program.

He told me that Ken Johansson had put a manual together and had done some good work with the volunteers, and that the under-20 national team program was just going to start, and this was something I could really help develop.

He liked the fact that I was close to Europeans, with Tarasov as a friend, and I was close to the Canadians, whom I met through my coaching in Austin. They wanted me to "run that under-20 national program and get it established, and develop a coaching program, and bring what-ever other ideas" that I had to develop American hockey.

I told Bob that we needed some sort of a development program, which would allow us to have hands-on time with our best young players. I thought camps for those young players would work and I knew that the US Olympic Committee was already thinking along those lines for all sports. I wanted to create a situation where the Olympic Committee would pay room and board at the Olympic Training Center for eighty kids of ours, along with the ice time for a camp in Colorado Springs.

Bob thought my ideas were good. He told me he had the opportunity to see my work for three years, and he had seen how I had built "a won-derful hockey team." He knew local kids in Rochester who had played on my teams and who had enjoyed the brand of hockey we produced. "I think you would be a breath of fresh air to get this project off the ground," he said.

I told Bob the philosophy that I learned from Anatoly Tarasov, just so he would be clear as to what I was bringing to the party. I told him that "Tarasov had taught me not to copy Canadians, or Russians, as we'll never beat them doing that. He said to make the ideas that you like in other countries into your own, and plug them into your own culture, and let them flourish."

Bob appreciated the philosophy. He said that it made a lot of sense. But he was also aware that making the United States into a competitive hockey country was not going to happen overnight. I told him that it would take twenty or thirty years before we would see the fruits of our labor, but we had to get going now.

You know, people tell you on a Tuesday that they'll start next Mon-day. I say that when you know what you need to do, then start right away. If you really want to lose weight, start right now and you'll be at the weight you want by next Christmas, or whenever your target date is.

It's the same thing with hockey. If you want to do something, you must start now and be prepared to suffer until you reach your goal, and then set a new one. Bob was impressed with it all, and I was impressed with dinner, which was delicious. We had a fine start. And I was very interested in the mission Bob had proposed.

The next day I got a call from Hal Trumble, the executive director of AHAUS. He said that he and the president of AHAUS, William Thayer Tutt, whom everyone called Thayer, wanted me to fly to Colorado Springs and spend the weekend. They would put me up at the Broadmoor hotel, which I didn't know at the time, but very much came to appreciate, was an exclusive and beautiful five-star resort. They would show me their office and introduce me to people, and we would talk more about my vision for the organization.

After two days of seeing things in Colorado Springs and telling them what I thought, Hal asked me, "Do you want to take on this challenge and move to Colorado?" I told him that I was definitely considering it, but I loved my teams. Now I even loved Austin, Minnesota. I wasn't sure.

He replied that he understood, and then went to the heart of the matter, as he saw it. He told me that I wasn't going to make any money there, of which I was well aware. I told him what I earned in Austin, and he said that he didn't know how I could live on it. I explained that I worked at hockey schools in the summer, and that I taught cooking classes and that I painted houses. I even worked on a farm for three days picking up rocks to earn some extra cash. But it was worth it.

He reminded me that I had a car that I had to stop every 10 miles to put in brake fluid. I told him that I couldn't afford to get rid of it. He had a solution. He offered me $9,000 a year ($43,000 today)[2] to start, and then they would review my work after a couple of months and would bump my salary up if all was well. "I think you'll like it." Hal said. "It's a great place to live, Lou. I live here now. We have a winter that lasts two or three weeks." He was from Minnesota, and I had endured several Minnesota winters, so I appreciated his point.

I left my luxurious resort in Colorado Springs, and I went back to my cottage in Austin, and I spoke to my friends there, who all understood that I had to make that move to Colorado Springs. So I went west.

After two months in the new job, I did get a raise to $10,000 (or nearly $48,000).[3] They couldn't have been nicer to me. There were just four of us there when I began, and today I think they have more than a hundred employees. But that is how I became involved with USA Hockey.

And of course, I got to meet people like Herb Brooks and Bob Johnson, two hockey guys who would have immense influence on me. They're two of the all-time great coaches in American hockey, and I got to work with both of them extensively.

John Mariucci was really a huge help to me. People call me the godfather of US hockey, but I would say that he is the real godfather. He was born in 1916 and had grown up in the Great Depression in Minnesota. He lived in Eveleth, in the northern part of the state, and they had excellent hockey rinks. So he played, but he didn't start organized hockey until he was a high school junior. He skated for hours on his own on the natural ice that surrounded him.

And when he started playing hockey on a team, he was a natural. He wound up playing at the University of Minnesota, and from there, played five seasons as a defenseman for the Chicago Black Hawks in the NHL.

Then he went to work on hockey in the United States after he hung up his skates for the NHL in 1950. He became a coach at the University of Minnesota in 1952 and led their team to second place in the NCAA tournament. He guided the US Olympic hockey team to a silver medal in the 1956 Olympic Games in Italy.

Mariucci believed in developing American players, and that's what he did. He coached at Minnesota for fourteen seasons, and in that time, he developed hockey at the high school and college level in Minnesota. He did there what I aimed to do for the country, and he was very effective.

In his time, they built more than one hundred full-size indoor rinks in Minnesota. They started hockey camps in the summer. They registered 80,000 amateur players. And they created leagues for kids as young as six years old and travel teams for ten-year-olds. Like Lloyd Percival tells us at the beginning of *The Hockey Handbook,* Mariucci knew where hockey success always began. "Everyone wants to play," he said, "but you can't play until you've learned to skate."[4]

John Mariucci was very kind to me when I was in Minnesota, and he is a very important guy in the story of American hockey, because his vision for Minnesota became mine for the country. I knew that we needed to produce a comprehensive manual for hockey coaches and play-ers alike to all get on the same page, as it were, but it was an expensive proposition.

From the get-go, I saw the world that I had entered could offer me the most unexpected adventures. I went to the first-ever college Hobey Baker awards banquet in Minnesota shortly after I started working for AHAUS. Gordie Howe was there, with his wife, Colleen. He introduced himself to me, and so began our friendship.

I mean, he needed no introduction. I had watched him play for the Red Wings from the balcony of Madison Square Garden from my $2 seats. I had marveled at his talent. And now, here he was standing in front of me, telling me that he was going to get himself a beer and asking me if he could get me a beer, too. Of course, I said yes.

At AHAUS I worked with the Europeans and the Canadians, and one of the guys I really liked was Dennis McDonald, who wound up being the general manager of the Winnipeg Jets, but at the time, in the later 1970s, he was running the coaching program in Canada. I met with Dennis, and I said, "Dennis, with all the manuals and stuff you're doing and I'm doing, what if we do them together? We could cut the price in half. I'll give you my input, you give me your input, and then it'll become a stronger coaching manual."

He wanted to do it, but the Canadian leadership didn't want to join forces with us. We would have saved a lot of money. I think they were wary of me because they knew that I liked the hockey style of the Euro-peans and the Soviets—especially the Soviets. I tried to tell them that a lot of the stuff that influenced the Soviets came from a Canadian, Lloyd Percival. He was a terrific hockey man and a great sports physiologist. Anatoly Tarasov could not have had more respect for the man, and yet he's hardly known today.

Lloyd Percival was fantastic. And I heard from the Hall of Famer Detroit Red Wings Ted Lindsay, and Gordie Howe, how highly they respected him. He worked with the Red Wings when he was considered an oddball by the Canadian sports establishment. He inspired me when I first read *The Hockey Handbook* in Brooklyn, and to this day, I still believe and do some of the things that were in that book.

I was actually laughed at by the great Bob Johnson when I told him that players don't have to stretch. "Bob," I said, "all they have to do is carry their bag into the locker room and they're ready to play." That was Lloyd Percival's teaching and it infuriated Bob.

In physiology, I had never heard of the oblique muscles, and I still don't even know what they are. Well, I do, as they're the muscles that connect the ribs, top of the hip bone, and lower back, and you use them in bending, twisting, and breathing. However, I think the reason today that we have a lot of injuries in sports is because the stretching of muscles, which can give you a bigger range of motion, but might weaken the muscle and not strengthen it, and as a result, I do not use stretching exercises in my training.[5]

Another thing I heard was never to let your players go into a deep squat. They will damage their knees. When I was in the Soviet Union, all they did was the deep squat, constantly jumping up and squatting down with their arms wrapped around medicine balls. And here's our doctor telling me that we can't do it.

When I was in the Soviet Union, I asked Tarasov about it. Don't these guys ever hurt their knees from this exercise? And he looked at me and said "*Nyet!*" He told me that they strengthened the players' legs and their entire lower body from the waist down.

"We spend most of our time strengthening that," he said. "You guys just spend time training from the waist up to get big muscles, right? You don't need to have big necks and big arms to be a hockey player. You need to be strong from the waist down!"

I was thinking about baseball catchers of the day, like Johnny Bench, and Yogi Berra, some of the greatest catchers in the history of baseball. They didn't miss games with knee injuries, and all they did was squat for two hundred days a year, doing deep squats up and down between pitches. I got to know Yogi Berra and I asked him if he ever had knee injury problems, and I related how forbidden squats were in hockey. He said, "No, Lou. I was tired once in a while, but that's about it." It's all very interesting to me.

In 1979, I got to bring my old pal Anatoly Tarasov over to the United States for an eighteen-city tour in which Tarasov would put on hockey clinics. He would actually be my guest in America three times, and I would stay at his flat in Moscow or at his dacha. We once got drunk there and fell asleep on the grass. His wife came out and sprinkled water on us and said "Time to get up boys." We did. We had a wonderful friendship.

On that trip in 1979 we were in Niagara Falls. I said, "Let's go see the Falls," and Tarasov and Arkady Chernyshev, another top Russian hockey guy, and Lev, our interpreter, were with me. So we were looking at Niagara Falls, a world-famous natural wonder. Tarasov would argue with me all the time, so he said, "Hmm, I thought I was going to see something special. We have better ones in the Soviet Union."

And I would have a go back at him, and say, "So is that why you built the wall in Berlin? To keep the West out? You don't want us to see these falls?"

We would have these daily battles, and Chernyshev would do his best to create peace. He would say to Tarasov, "Why do you insult the host every day?" and Tarasov would just grin.

Then we went downstairs to the aquarium at Niagara Falls. The dolphins were doing their tricks, and we were watching them. Tarasov said something to Lev the interpreter and to Chernyshev. And they all laughed. So I said "Well, what did he say?"

The interpreter didn't want to tell me, but Tarasov insisted that he do so. Lev said, "Tarasov told me that you Americans amaze him. You have such beautiful supermarkets with so much fruit and food and good buildings and nice waterfalls, and many beautiful things. You can even teach fish to perform the most difficult tasks. Tell me, why can't you teach a hockey player to make a pass stick to stick?"

He was such a fine coach. I said, "Your defensemen are so good at stripping the opponent of the puck without having to take the body out." And he smiled and said, "You do wasteful exercises in Canada. I'll show you how it's done."

On the ice, he would have pucks scattered around, and he had three groups of forwards and a defenseman waiting for his command. He would blow the whistle and one of the groups of forwards would pick up a puck and come at the defenseman. The defenseman didn't know which of the three groups of forwards was going to come at him at high speed.

His instruction from Tarasov was to stop all three groups, but for the first few times, he couldn't stop anybody. But they kept going and before you knew it, he had stopped all three groups. They would do this drill for a half hour, and that's how they learned to strip the puck without taking the body.

Tarasov's trip to North America almost didn't happen. I was sitting at the table in Moscow, at a meeting at Luzhniki Arena, with my executive director Hal Trumble and Thayer Tutt, the president of AHAUS. Thayer was a very kind guy in his late sixties who had helped bring the Soviet Union ice hockey team to the United States for the first time in 1959, and he loved the game. We were there to hash out the details of the trip and this Vyacheslav Koloskov was canceling the trip. I said, "You can't cancel it, the word is out already."

I'll never forget that room. It was a nice pine wood room, but they had three dead flowers in a vase in the middle of the table. And there were two pictures on the wall, one of Castro and one of Brezhnev. It set the tone.

Koloskov was a physiologist who became president of the Soviet Soccer Federation. He was a sports bureaucrat. I asked Tarasov about him, and he said, "He's a very educated man. He's scientific. He's smart. And he's worth listening to. But he's not practical. He's a theorist. Everything he says looks beautiful on paper, but it's not always practical. He doesn't know how to deal with practicality. But you should listen to him when he talks and then shake your head, yes. And do what you want after because he doesn't know how to deal with people."

So I listened to his impracticality, and then I did not shake my head in agreement. Instead I said again, "Listen, you can't cancel it. It's already been advertised." And he said to me, "We can't help if Mr. Tarasov is ill and can't travel."

I knew, upon hearing that lie, that I had him. Because Koloskov didn't know that Tarasov was at the game in the very arena where we were meeting. Tarasov had seen me enter the arena earlier and he went wild. He gave me a big hug and a kiss and took me over to the snack bar, to sit down with other old Soviet players. We ate and drank and talked. He was hale and hearty and not at all ill.

Tarasov said to me, "Lou, they're trying to hurt me personally. They won't let me leave the country to do this trip. There's nothing wrong with me. Here I am. Look!" And he poured vodka while he was talking, and drank a lot of it. He said, "They just don't want me to go."

So I knew this already when the big Communist Koloskov told me that Tarasov was ill and in the hospital. I said, "Are you sure he's in the hospital?" He said to me, "Are you calling me a liar?" And I looked him right in the eye in front of all these important sports people. I said, "One hundred percent I'm calling you a liar. I'm disgusted with the audacity you have to lie to us like this." He was surprised and he did not like hearing this. But I was on a roll.

I said, "Here's the problem with you Soviets. Here's how you negotiate. 'What's mine is mine. What's yours we'll negotiate.' So if you want to do that, here's how it is going to go. You cannot play a hockey game in the United States of America ever without our permission. You can't play NHL teams exhibition games in the USA if we don't okay it. And I'm hoping my federation has the courage to do the right thing and deny your Soviet teams. The first trip they made to North America was to Colorado Springs. It wasn't to Toronto, or to Montreal. It was to Colorado Springs and Thayer Tutt took great care of all of you. And this is the thanks we get. You're lying to me."

He said, "How dare you accuse me of lying!"

I said, "Gentlemen, would you like to walk with me to greet Mr. Tarasov? He's in this arena, having shots of vodka and bantering with old-time Soviet players. I just had lunch with him."

There was silence in the room. Then Thayer Tutt said, "Lou, I know you're upset. I think it'd be a good idea if you stepped out of this room for a while. Go cool off."

I went out of the room, and 20 minutes later Thayer came out and brought me back in. Now everybody was smiling and there were bottles of vodka and glasses on the table and they were making ridiculous phony toasts about peace and brotherhood. I almost said something, but Thayer had his hand behind my back, and he pinched me. It was a pinch that said "Keep your mouth shut."

Koloskov had changed his tone as easily as he blinked. "Look, since we didn't know Tarasov had made such a good recovery from his hospital stay," which he had not done because he had not been ill or in the hospital to begin with, "here's our proposal. It was accepted by Mr. Trumble, Mr. Fleming, and Mr. Bush, and the proposal is that he can go but you have to bring Arkady Chernyshev with him. And if you really know the history of our hockey, Chernyshev was much more important to the development of hockey in the Soviet Union." And I got pinched in the back again. So all I said was "Okay."

So that's how I got Tarasov to come present his dryland clinics across the country. Chernyshev was a surprise, and we hit it off big time. Tarasov was a showman. And Chernyshev was a total professor, a gentleman, who was very well spoken, and very honest.

Chernyshev told me stories on the trip. He said he had never been a member of the Communist Party. He didn't like what they did to members of his family. He wasn't afraid. He was sponsored by the KGB, because he coached Moscow Dynamo, and they were a KGB program. He was a great coach and just as fine a guy.

But if I hadn't put my foot down and did what I did, that eighteen-city trip would not have happened. If you confront people who are cowards and bullies head on, they will melt.

At the end of the 1970s, I was trying to get USA Hockey off the ground, so to speak. There were just four of us buzzing in the office, but we did not have a lot of money, and we couldn't do programs that we wanted to do. Even so, I was just relentless in my desire to make the game of hockey better for American players.

In my first year with USA Hockey (still AHAUS, but not for long), we tried a development camp with kids who came from the Pacific Division. It was shocking to see that there were kids this good coming from Alaska and California, and there weren't a lot of them, but one of them was Chris Chelios, and there were a few others from Portland and different places not known as hockey hotbeds. We ran that camp for a week up in Squaw Valley, California, in that gorgeous outdoor rink in the mountains where the 1960 Winter Olympics were held.

I knew that we needed to create a national development camp for fifteen- and sixteen-year-olds, and I loved what we had accomplished with the Pacific kids in Squaw Valley. I was really frustrated that I couldn't get some of these programs going.

I managed to get the coaching program going immediately, as that was an easier task, recruiting and training hockey coaches locally. But I couldn't get the national development camp program going, and it was a challenge to me.

I had never worked in an office, so I wasn't familiar with all the paperwork. Back then, we had no electronic wizardry to transmit ideas. For anything that you wanted to propose at AHAUS, you had to write your idea by hand on a form. The form asked the basic questions: What? Why? When? Where? Who? And of course, the kicker, which was How Much? How much would your great idea cost AHAUS, which had no money. So I started writing.

Next to What? I wrote "National Camp for 15- and 16-year-olds."

When? "Summer offseason."

Why? "To identify and develop our best players from around the country."

And then I wrote more, speaking directly and bluntly to my boss, Hal Trumble. "I'm from New York City. We have good hockey players coming up in New York City. New York State has excellent hockey players, too. You're from Minnesota, Hal, and you think everything there is perfect. This is the Amateur Hockey Association of the United States, not the Amateur Hockey Association of Minnesota and it's pissing me off."

Yes, I wrote that down, and I wasn't finished. "Kids can play hockey from anywhere if given an opportunity. We, as the governing body, should be giving a fair opportunity to all of our members, not just the best players from Minnesota. I lived there and coached there. I love your state. And I never had a bad kid from Minnesota ever. They could all play hockey and they were all good kids. Kids from New York City might be a little rougher, but they can play hockey too, if given the chance."

Hal would come into the office in the morning and take all of the idea and recommendation forms out of the box, and he would read them with his red pencil in hand (just like Tarasov). He would not go home until he was done marking them up with his thoughts. He looked at my long recommendation form, and he circled the word "Budget" in red and then wrote "See me."

I went to see him. He told me, "Lou, we're not going to do it. We don't have the money. We're just now starting to get a couple of sponsors."

I pushed back hard. I said, "We have to do this. We can't lose this entire year. We have to start the program. We have to find out who can play hockey across all fifty states. We have to have at least one kid from the southeast region. We have to have one from Alaska. The Pacific. The Midwest—you don't think there's a player in Indiana? Nevada? Montana? I mean, if they play hockey in these places, there's got to be at least one talented kid. And they're going to come here, play hockey, then go home aware that other kids across the country are also good at hockey, and it is going to create a national community which is going to make us better."

He thought about that, and I could see that he didn't disagree. He said, "How would you break down the country into the eighty kids at this camp?"

In those days, we had team registrations and not those for individual players. The state that had the most teams was Minnesota. I said, "So we'll figure out the percentage. If they have 70 percent of the teams in the country or 30 percent, they'll get that percentage." There were twelve districts, plus Alaska, and I thought everybody should have at least one representative.

He nodded, but again told me that it was going to cost a fortune. A fortune we did not have. I told him that I had called the Olympic Committee, and that they would give us a week's residence at their training center. We could hold the camp at their rink, which was two blocks from the training center, and they would pay for the ice time. They were all in. The players had to get there on their own.

Hal wanted to know who would be working with me at this development camp, and I told him that if our coaching program directors were good enough to teach our coaches, then they were good enough to help in this camp. And best of all, they were all volunteers. We could offer them free room and board to come help these young players, and I knew that they would love to be a part of it. I could discuss the coaching program with them while they were in town with me, so we would accomplish a lot in one go.

He thought some more, then shook his head and addressed a specific point in my note to him that I had written on the form. "No, we're not going to do it. I don't believe there are players in New York City that can play."

I was exasperated. I told him that I knew there were good players in New York City, and in fact, I knew a really good young player who would be perfect, a kid named Joe Mullen. I played roller hockey with his father. Today, Joe Mullen is in the Hockey Hall of Fame. He scored 502 goals in the NHL.

In truth, Hal was worried about the finances more than anything else. He liked the idea, but the money was stopping him. So I took a gamble and made it even more personal. I said, "You know what you are, Hal, you're a Minnesota prick. And I don't care if you fire me. I'll go back to Minnesota and coach. I don't mean to be rude to you. I like you. I respect you. But you're really wrong. And we're not going to get better if we don't include the whole country."

And he said, "Okay. Very good. Maybe I want to be a prick."

I said, "You're doing a good job of it."

Then I walked out and went back to my office.

Our conversation was very early in the morning, and at about 8 a.m., two hours after it ended, I got a call from Hal. He wasn't firing me, but instead he was inviting me to go to lunch with him at the Broadmoor golf club. The president of AHAUS, Thayer Tutt, would be there, and we were going to discuss my idea. Hal had heard me.

Thayer was a wonderful man. I explained everything to him. He heard me, too.

And he said, "Well, I believe I can get a grant. If you have the room and board covered, and all the other expenses, I can come up with the rest. How much do you think we'll need?"

I said that we could probably do it for $15,000. His eyes went wide, and he said, how much?

I thought we were done for, but I told him again that it would cost $15,000.

He said "Christ, I thought it would be a lot more than that."

He took out his checkbook and he wrote a check to AHAUS for $15,000.

He said, "Here you go, boys. Do a good job now, and I want to come down and watch some of it." And that's how that happened.

Thayer died in 1989, so he didn't live long enough to see how good we became as a country at hockey. Just look at the players in the NHL today. We have players from every state, almost, not just Minnesota, which is still number one, but not by a lot.

I think they have one or two more players than New York State, which produces wonderful players. And so it all worked out, and it was, to me, one of the proudest things I've ever been involved in.

At that first camp, we had a kid named Johnston from Alabama. He probably was the weakest kid there. But he wasn't bad. At that time, they had one rink in the state. He became the president of the kids youth minor hockey organization in Alabama. He's a grandfather now, but what we did had a far-reaching effect, bringing all these different kids together from all over the country.

We still do it today, but we have three or four age groups. We have the national team development program at Ann Arbor, which came out of what we did. Now that I had been part of starting that monumental development in American hockey, I would get my next shot to prove that we could play hockey with the best at the Winter Olympics of 1980. It would become famous as "the Miracle on Ice." Let me tell you, and I will, that there was nothing miraculous about it.

The Miracle on Ice

I WANT TO TELL YOU A STORY ABOUT HOW USA HOCKEY GOT ITS NAME. As I mentioned, it was called the Amateur Hockey Association of the United States and it was a terrible, clunky kind of name, with an even worse acronym, AHAUS, which sounds like a sneeze. When Badger Bob Johnson was fired as the coach of the Calgary Flames in 1987, he wound up working at AHAUS, as the executive director. He was in the office when the receptionist answered the phone and said, "Good afternoon, Amateur Hockey Association of the United States. How may I help you?"

As soon as she was done, Bob said, "From now on you answer the phone 'USA Hockey.'" Then he went to his office, and he called the president, Walter Bush. And Bob Johnson said, "We have to change our name right now to USA Hockey." The president said that he had to convene a meeting of the board to make such a momentous decision. Bob said, "I'm calling it USA Hockey from now on." The president made a few calls, and everybody approved the new name and that's how it came about. Bob had heard enough and changed it. No forms involved.

How I came to join the Olympic team in 1980 is actually a journey that started in Minnesota. When I was coaching the junior team in Austin, Minnesota, my phone rang one day. The person on the other end asked to speak to me and I admitted that I was Lou Vairo and that he could go ahead. And he said, "Hi, Lou. My name is Herb Brooks. And I coach hockey at the U." I hadn't been in Austin very long, so I said, "What's the U?" I didn't know what the U was.

He said "What?" with this tone of incredulity.

I said again, "What's the U, Mr. Brooks?" He said, "The University of Minnesota!" He was suddenly agitated, and thought I was mocking him.

I said to him, "Easy, easy. How am I supposed to know that? The only colleges I know about are City College in New York and Brooklyn College. Do you know about them? Do you know where Brooklyn College is?"

He said that he did not, so I told him that I had not meant to insult him, and that now I knew what I had not known moments earlier. I said, "The U must be the nickname for the University of Minnesota," and he said no, it was not. The Golden Gophers was the nickname. It was becoming a bit of a comedy routine, but we eventually got to the point of his call.

He said, "I've seen two of your practices. And I saw your team play an exhibition game. And I liked what I saw very, very much. You're going to do a good job. It reminded me of Soviet hockey. And here's what I'd like to offer you. Two tickets to every home game at the U. You can use them however you want. You can give the tickets to any of your players. We're also going to be scouting your team, looking for players for the U."

I was happy to hear all of this, and then he went one better. He told me that they had a junior varsity hockey team at the U that was as good as most other universities' varsity squads. "I'd like to invite your team up here as we have a free Monday night at Williams Arena. And I know that you usually have a day off Monday for your team. But if you want, your guys are welcome to come up every Monday and play us. I can scout your players that way. And it'd be good for them to play the kind of competition that we'd offer them."

So I said, "That offer sounds great. Thank you very much."

We went up to the U to play the Golden Gophers' junior varsity squad about six times, which was an excellent opportunity for our team to test itself against these older college guys. And Herb Brooks would be there. He was very nice to me. And respectful. And so we developed a little bit of a friendship. When he was at home and we were playing, he would come to our junior games in the Twin Cities. He would come to practices as well. He would take notes as he watched the game or the practice. He would not always come to speak to me, so as not to disrupt my coaching rhythm. He would just quietly come in and watch. That's how I got to know Herb Brooks, sometimes close up, sometimes from a distance.

I also had found out by then his Minnesota hockey pedigree. He had been born in St. Paul in 1937, and had played hockey in high school, winning the state championship with his team as a forward. He played for the University of Minnesota and had almost made it to the 1960 Winter Olympics where the United States won hockey gold, but Brooks was the last man cut from the team. He had to watch them win the gold medal on TV, but it didn't discourage him. He only worked harder, and played for the US national team eight times, including on the Olympic hockey teams in 1964 and 1968.

He became a coach and led the University of Minnesota hockey team to two national championships, in 1972 and 1974, with a third to come in 1979. He was a very good hockey player, and an even better hockey coach.

When I went to work for AHAUS, he wrote a very nice letter to me, including a picture of the University of Minnesota team national champions, and he wrote, "You're doing a great job for AHAUS, Lou. Keep it up, keep doing what you're doing. You're on the right track."

He was very supportive. And by now I knew who he was, and I respected him. However, he wouldn't do a lot of the things that I did with teams. In fact, most of the coaches didn't. They liked how my teams played. They came to our games, and they were nice to me. And they should have been nice to me because we played beautiful hockey. But they were afraid. They knew how to play my style of hockey, too, of puck possession and creativity, with less emphasis on punishing physicality and more on skill.

But a lot of these coaches did not have the courage to take the steps that I took. That was due to the fact that they wanted to coach in the NHL one day, and they didn't want to be seen as too "out of line." By that, I mean they didn't want to be perceived as being too far removed from the type of hockey that the NHL played. The dump and chase, and hit hard, and fight kind of hockey.

Coaching in the NHL was never on my mind because I had never planned to be a coach. If I had not gone to the USSR to the School of Tarasov, to learn from him, and if those coaches hadn't bailed on us at the rink in Flushing, Queens, I might never have become a coach. Certainly not the type I became. But to many of the coaches in the established, or establishment hockey coach club, I was straddling two hockey worlds, and they could only coach in one.

These coaches were really coaching to snag their next job in the big leagues, and there was nothing wrong with that. Their ambition was to coach in the NHL and it's a very worthy goal. I'm not criticizing it. However, they could have done more for their teams, and for themselves, but there was a risk involved, one that they did not want to take.

The hockey world in North America at the time was basically run by the old white man's Canadian Hockey Club. "If you can't beat them in the alley, you can't beat them on the ice," was their motto. It was almost a cliché, and created a game that relied more on the rough tough stuff than on creativity. These coaches didn't want to offend anybody in that club. So they wouldn't go as far as I went.

I didn't care what the club said. I cared what my players thought, and I cared about making them better, and I cared that they were having fun playing hockey. Herb Brooks had noticed me and my teams because we were good, and different, and our relationship grew over time. He would often call me and ask me my opinion on things. "Did you see this game or that game that we played last night?" Or "I'm having trouble with so and so, what would you do?"

He was secretive. He never admitted he was consulting with me, because he was almost embarrassed to admit that he was asking a roller hockey guy from Brooklyn ice hockey questions. I was never offended. But he saw my value, so that's how I came to get picked to be on the 1980 Olympic team coaching staff.

But I was not staff, as I was not officially on the list, as they say. I think Herb Brooks thought of me as some kind of experimental device he could use to gain an advantage on the teams that the United States was playing. I was a "technical advisor." Here's how it all came about.

I was working for AHAUS in 1979 in Colorado Springs at the Air Force Academy, at what they called the National Olympic Sports Festival. It was the second one that the Olympic Committee had staged, and it was a good idea that I would borrow and use in summer camps.

The idea behind this event was that it would be a selection festival for Olympic athletes, taking place over six days in July and holding competitions in thirty-one Olympic sports.

The athletes were divided up by region, so we had Midwest, South, East, and West, but as the south didn't really exist yet in terms of hockey, the hockey component of the festival was divided into New England, Great Lakes, Midwest, and Central. The teams would train and then play a round-robin tournament at the Broadmoor Arena, and from that, twenty-six players would be selected for the men's Olympic hockey team.

Herb had been selected to coach that Olympic hockey team so he would be there every day, watching the teams, as would I. While we were watching the game, he would ask me what I thought of various players, and I would tell him. He had an advisory committee with him, but I was never invited to speak to the committee. It was just Herb and me, one on one, before or after he met with the committee.

We both liked similar players, and Herb knew that the hockey of tomorrow was going to be different than the hockey of today. He also knew that my teams were trying to play the hockey of tomorrow. And we were winning.

In the final game, the team from Great Lakes came back from being down 2–0 in the first period with a pair of goals by Ken Morrow to beat the Midwest 4–2 and win the championship at the festival. And from those teams, Herb Brooks had to pick his Olympic squad.[1]

Herb picked twenty-six players, but as he said at the time, he could have picked thirty-six, or even forty-six.[2] He said, "We'll pick the twenty final players from this group, and then I will add six more," but Mike Eruzione, one of the players selected, knew of this plan and told Herb he couldn't bring in new players. He couldn't cut some players and add others. The team knew it as well, and if he had done it, there would have been trouble.

Herb called me one Sunday morning and asked what he should do. I told him to leave the team alone. "You can't break your word. And that's not who you are." That killed his ill-advised plan, and he didn't make any changes to the roster. He kept the team he had picked at Colorado Springs, which was exactly the right thing to do.

And then I became part of it. Herb said to me, "We play Sweden first. What I'd love you to do, Lou, is to come to the Olympics and go upstairs with a walkie-talkie connected to Craig Patrick on the bench and tell him what you see. You'll meet with me every morning. And every evening." And then he laid out that while I would be working with Team USA, I wouldn't actually be on it. "You can't stay in the village, and I can't put you on the staff," he said, "and I'm not sure this walkie-talkie thing is even legal, I imagine it is, but I don't know. I don't want to risk anything."

We had to check to see if the use of walkie-talkies to communicate was legal, and it was. Even so, we had to get a license for it, to make it official, so that when people saw me on a walkie-talkie, they didn't think I was some kind of spy. I was one of the early analysts in the sky, watching the action down below.

That was Herb's plan. He wanted me to come down to ice level after each period and meet him outside the dressing room and give him an analysis of what I had seen from my perch above. I have no idea how much I helped that team, but I could see that they were a comprehensive team who had the talent to win it all.

Herb became much more advanced as a coach with that Olympic team, but Craig Patrick deserves a lot of credit for the 1980 Olympic team's success. Herb was still struggling with relationships with players. He was a little distant. He was the right hockey coach, and a very talented hockey man, but a little bit aloof. Craig Patrick was a man of the people.

Craig was his assistant coach, and he was the perfect guy for that job. The players loved him and respected him. He came with an impeccable hockey pedigree, hailing from the greatest hockey family in NHL history. Lester Patrick was his grandfather, and Frank Patrick was his great-uncle. Lynn Patrick, who played for the New York Rangers for ten seasons, was his father, and Muzz (who played with his brother Lynn for the Blueshirts, and together won the Stanley Cup in 1940) was his uncle. All of them are members of the Hockey Hall of Fame.

In fact, Frank and Lester Patrick were responsible for much of what Herb Brooks and I and everyone else who played hockey in 1980 was doing on the ice. In 1911, the Patrick brothers formed the Pacific Coast Hockey Association with teams on the west coast, in Vancouver, British Columbia, its suburb New Westminster, and in Victoria, on Vancouver Island. They would add teams in Seattle and Portland as they brought hockey to the western United States, and they did it on artificial ice.

The Patricks' ice rink in Vancouver was the largest artificial ice arena in the world, beating Madison Square Garden by 500 seats. They did not invent artificial ice, but they used it to bring hockey to a region that didn't have much of the natural stuff in winter. And then they went to work.

The Patrick brothers, and their Pacific league, gave hockey numbered jerseys, which they had seen on the backs of cross-country runners in a British magazine. They created line changes and allowed goalies to fall to the ice to make saves—until then, they had to stand up—and frustrated by offside calls, they divided the ice into three zones with forward passing allowed inside this offensive zone, and so the blue line came to be. They also created a playoff system. In 1915, their team the Vancouver Millionaires won the Stanley Cup. The Patricks were more than hockey royalty: they were hockey wizards.[3]

Craig was a very important part of that 1980 team, and Herb was the coach, and I wanted to support them both. Every coach is insecure to some extent. I was, Tarasov was, and every coach is. It's a very difficult job to be head coach of a high-level sports team. Even coaching a peewee team has its stresses. You ask yourself: am I really doing a good job? How can I do it better? You blame yourself for losses, and sometimes are surprised by the wins. It's a stressful life.

So Herb really wanted me to support him by following the Swedish team and then telling him what I saw. In fact, it would turn out to be more than that. I told Herb that I needed permission from my boss at AHAUS, so Herb said he would call Hal. Then Hal called me and told me what I was going to do, which made my Olympic job even better. "I'm bringing you to Lake Placid anyway," he said. "You're going to be the team host of Sweden. You'll meet them at Kennedy Airport and here's the date that they're coming in. You know, Lindstrom, the team leader," whom I did know and who was a great guy. "And Tommy Sandlin is the coach." I knew Tommy as well, and so I said that I would do it. Then Hal laid out the plan.

"They get to play an exhibition game, and two or three friendly matches. And you'll hang out with them, and you'll be their host for approximately fifteen days."

I told Herb Brooks, and he was happy with that plan, as it put me deep inside the enemy camp because the Swedes had a very fine hockey team. They were the team to beat. So I met the Swedes at JFK, and we drove up to New Hampshire on the bus, and I was their host all the way through their time in New Hampshire during the 1980 Winter Olympics.

We even stopped in Boston, on our drive down from Dartmouth to Lake Placid, and I was able to get a little discount on hockey tickets. Toronto was playing in Boston, and the Swedish team wanted to see their fellow Swede, Borje Salming, who was playing for the Maple Leafs. I took them to that game, and they loved it, even if the Bruins won it 8–6.[4]

I had a very good relationship with Team Sweden, and I watched every practice that they had and every game that they played. And what I saw was hockey at its finest. There was no Swede who couldn't skate. I don't remember any player ever missing a pass in every practice and in every game. They beat Dartmouth College 21–0 in an exhibition game.

They had a hell of a team. Mats Naslund was on the team, and he would go on to star for the Montreal Canadiens. Pelle Lindbergh was in goal, and he would star for the Philadelphia Flyers, as would Tomas Eriksson. Tomas Jonsson would go on to play for the Islanders, with whom he won the Stanley Cup. They had many fine players.

Herb then wanted me to go to Montreal and check out the Canadian team, so I rented a car—and I don't know how I got there because I can get lost even in a one-street town—and I found my way to the old Montreal Forum. I watched Canada and the Czechs and two other teams play pre-Olympic Games. Then I drove back to Lake Placid, which was a little over an hour's drive from Montreal.

I already had a line on these other teams, and they were all very good, but our first opponent was Sweden. Herb and I met in Lake Placid as soon as I got back, and he wanted to know what I had seen. Now when I scouted and even when I coached, I picked one or two or, at the maximum, three items that we should really pay attention to. I didn't flood the coaches' or players' minds with thirty things and a lot of gibberish.

Herb and Craig are very smart, and they saw what I saw. But I had a better vantage point than them and total focus, as I just had to watch the game, and they had to coach a team. They had to worry about changing lines and matching lines, and on the bench, you don't see what you can see 40 feet up from the ice.

I saw the whole rink. It was perfect. During the games that the United States played, I would only speak occasionally to Craig via the walkie-talkie. When I saw something that I thought was really important I would tell them, like a shift in tactics or player adjustments. Usually, Herb and Craig had seen it too.

I think my value was coming down in between each period. After the first period we played against Sweden, I was all excited and I ran down the steps, which wasn't too far because it's a small rink in Lake Placid. And we met in a hallway outside the dressing room that was private. Herb would lift up his right foot and lean against the wall, and I'd stand in front of him, and he'd ask questions, or I would tell him something that I thought was important. But after that first period against Sweden, he was so nervous. He was cursing. "That damn Kenny Johansson," he said, about the former GM. "I told him the schedule was too tough. But dammit, the Swedes are going to run us out of the building. We can't skate with them."

I had told him how good the Swedes were, but now he finally understood. He said, "Lou, you're right. They are the most skilled team in this tournament. They're more skilled than the Russians." That's really how he was—he could go from confidence to disaster in a heartbeat, and I could see that his realization of how good the Swedish team really was had deflated him. I said, "Herb, get hold of yourself. We're tied 1–1. I do think that they are the most skilled team. But the Czechs are going to be tough, and the Soviets beat us 10–3 in an exhibition game at Madison Square Garden. I didn't see the game. You were there. You know."

He looked at me and shook his head. "We could skate with those guys." I told him that I knew that. I said, "Herb, we just skated with Sweden."

"No!" he said. "They were faster."

I realized I had some work to do to put this in perspective or our coach would be a pile of mush by the end of the second period. I said, "It's our first game. Some of those kids playing for Sweden have played before in the Under-20 World Championships. Some played in the previous World Championships in 1976. They're really good. But so are we."

He said, "I don't know. Jesus. I think we're a tight team, and our schedule was too tough." I saw in his eyes the look of fear. I had to take dramatic action. I grabbed him by his lapels. I wasn't going to rough him up; I just wanted to shake him up a bit. And I said, "Look at me." He did, in astonishment. I said, "Herb, you have no idea what a great coach you are, how much I'm learning from you. You and Craig have done an incredible job with this hockey team. Stop thinking that way. We can medal"—I didn't say gold medal as I didn't want him to think I was crazy—and then I went for the jugular of the matter. "I love the way we played. We don't have to change a thing. Just keep playing. And believe in the team and believe in yourself. You have to know that you're a great coach!"

And you know what he said to me? His whole demeanor changed, and no one knows this story but me, because Herb passed away in 2003, and I was the only one there. And he spoke to me like he was a little boy in a soft, shy voice. He said, "You really think so? You mean that?"

I said, "One hundred percent."

He said, "Thank you, Lou." And then he and I went back to coaching.

I think I gave him some confidence. And we were lucky in that game. We got some bounces that went our way, and we ended up with a tie, but nobody knew how good Pelle Lindbergh would be in goal. I mean, I had never seen him play at this level, but we saw it during that game.

The game that fooled me the most was our match against Czechoslovakia. The night before that game, I took Karel Gut, their head coach, and his assistants Luděk Bukač and Stanislav Neveselý, who were all friends of mine from my work with AHAUS and coaching seminars, to the Italian house at Lake Placid.

I can speak fairly decent Italian, and I had made friends with the Italian house, and had brought them a little USA Hockey banner that they put up in their room. They were so proud of it. They would invite me to come and dine with them every day, and they had brought their own food and chefs and thousands of cases of wine from Italy, and so dining there was superb.

The Italians always told me to bring guests for dinner and it would always be free. So I brought the Czechs there to dine and they loved it. Who wouldn't? It was spectacular food and drink. And during dinner, Luděk Bukač said, "I watched your team practice today. Much too hard of a practice. I think your coaches made a mistake."

I said, "Herb's a great coach. He made no mistake. He knows his people just like you know yours."

"We wouldn't train like that," he said.

I said, "We'll find out tomorrow what's going to happen."

Stanislav Neveselý and I had a good friendship, and he had told me that they had special security with their team, and it bothered him. He told me that they were worried about their best players, the Stastnys, defecting to us. He was also worried about the loss of Ivan Hlinka, who had broken his leg. "He was the key man on our power play so we're scrambling a little bit," he said.

The Czechs did have an excellent team. They didn't have guys leaving them for the NHL quite yet, but they soon would, when Peter and Anton Stastny defected later that year to play for the Quebec Nordiques, to be followed the year after that by their brother Marian. They were a talented and proud team that represented two nationalities, the Czechs and the Slovaks. And we ran them out of the building.

We beat the Czechs 7–3, and I never would have expected that. I thought it would be a tight 2–2 or 3–3 game like we had played against Sweden. We played a very solid game and that was the key moment when I thought we could win it all. We could beat anyone.

The media kept calling our guys a "miracle" team. I would call them a great team, with many fine players. Goalie Jim Craig probably had the best three weeks of his life. He was a very good goalie, but he played out of his mind in those Olympic games. Our three top centermen were superb: Mark Johnson, Neal Broten, and Mark Pavelich. Mark Wells was our fourth centerman, and he had a job to do, and he did it well. For pure talent, I don't think any USA team has ever had three players like Neal Broten, Mark Johnson, and Mark Pavelich, who were absolute American hockey legends.

They were highly skilled, with more than an abundance of hockey sense, and they had great hands. And they could skate. They were highly underrated, all three of them. They were true Hall of Fame-level players. And they never got their due, in my opinion. Having said that, they should get their due. These were three of the greatest.

I coached every one of them along the way. I was either assistant coach or head coach with every one of them. These were players who didn't really need a coach. You just had to put them on the ice, and they could do it all. They could play against anybody, including the Soviets, and even outplay them.

And our defense was sensational. We were playing an exhibition game against Canada, who we struggled with every game. We never played them in the 1980 Olympic Games, thank God. They were tough. But we didn't have the depth. We had those three great players.

Herb was away with the team, and I spoke with him on the phone. He was worrying that we didn't have a defenseman who could lug the puck out of the zone and up the ice. Kenny Morrow could do it at times, but other than that, we had Mike Ramsey, who was a fine player, but he wasn't that good at carrying the puck out of our end.

Herb ran into a former Olympian who was our player David Christian's uncle. Everyone called the uncle "Skinny," so he was known as Skinny Christian. Herb ran into Skinny, and we had just lost to Canada in an exhibition game, and Herb was pacing and cursing and pissed off that our defensemen were not great at lugging the puck out of our zone. Skinny said, "Why don't you try David on defense?" Herb was incredulous. "He's a winger!"

Skinny shook his head. "He's not just a winger. He's a centerman, he's a defenseman, and if you need him in goal, he can do that, too."

David Christian was a wonderful hockey player, and Skinny said, "Herb, try David. He'll get the puck out of your end."

Herb continued to protest, so Skinny continued. "I was his coach in high school. He never came off the ice for one minute. He can play center if you need to plug him in. But he played D the whole game of every game that we played. If you freeze the Lake of the Woods, he can cover that 2,000 acres of lake in no time. He can skate backwards and forwards and sideways. Try him."

So Herb tried Dave on defense, and it's that story that's never been told. Dave was the difference. He made our team complete. So now we had Jack O'Callahan. We had Mike Ramsey, Billy Baker, Bobby Suter, and Ken Morrow, and we had Dave Christian. That'd be a tough lineup to face in the NHL right now. These guys were first-rate players.

We had beaten Norway, Romania, and Germany to have a record of four wins and one tie in the opening round. Now we were in the final round, and our opponents were the Soviets. It was the Cold War on ice all over again.

We got on the scoreboard first, thanks to our "Iron Range" line of Mark Pavelich, John Harrington, and Buzz Schneider who put us up 1–0. The Soviets quickly responded, tying the game three minutes later, and then they took the lead before Mark Johnson tied it up late in the period.

When the second period began, I was surprised to see that the Soviets had replaced their superb goalie Vladislav Tretiak with their backup goaltender Vladimir Myshkin. The Soviets took the lead again, but Mark Johnson tied it again midway through the third period with his second goal of the game.

Not too long after that, team captain Mike Eruzione scored for us, and goalie Jim Craig was a total star for the last 10 minutes under the Soviet onslaught. As it was clear that we were going to win, the broadcaster Al Michaels shouted, "Do you believe in miracles? . . . Yes!"

We had made it into the gold medal game, where Herb Brooks would say words to his team that still ring out loudly today. "You were born to be a player. You were meant to be here. This moment is yours." So it was, as we won that game, against Finland, and the gold medal.

Everyone recalls our win against the Soviets as a "miracle," but it was no miracle. We did not need divine intervention to beat them. We were that good. And we showed how good we were throughout the Olympics, starting with that tie against the Swedes.

And if I did anything to help us win, I think my greatest contribution was in helping Herb with his confidence. At least I believed in him, and he knew it. I think he respected and appreciated that. I don't want to take credit for anything else in that monumental victory. I was just happy to be asked to be a part of it.

Lou with his grandfather, Salvatore.
Collection of the author

Lou visiting Santa.
Collection of the author

Lou's parents and grandparents.
Collection of the author

Lou (*on the left*) with brother Jerry playing roller hockey in Brooklyn. *Collection of the author*

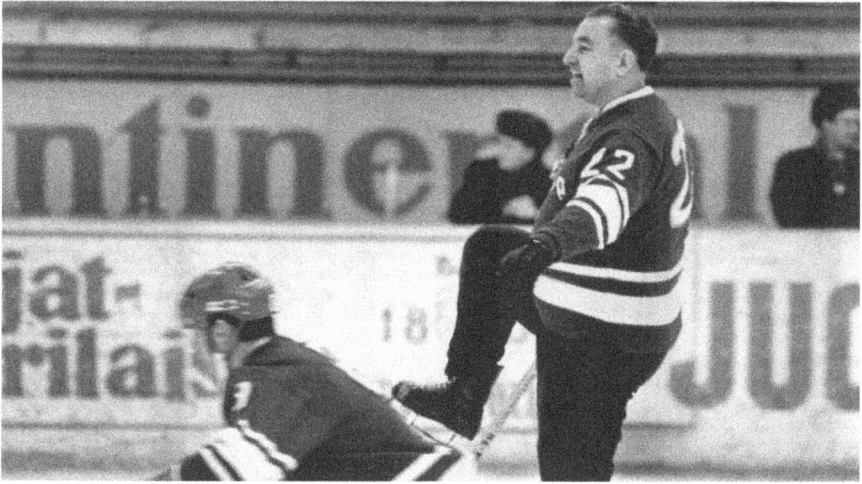

Anatoli Tarasov in Finland, 1970. *Photo by Veikko Lintinen/Lehtikuva*

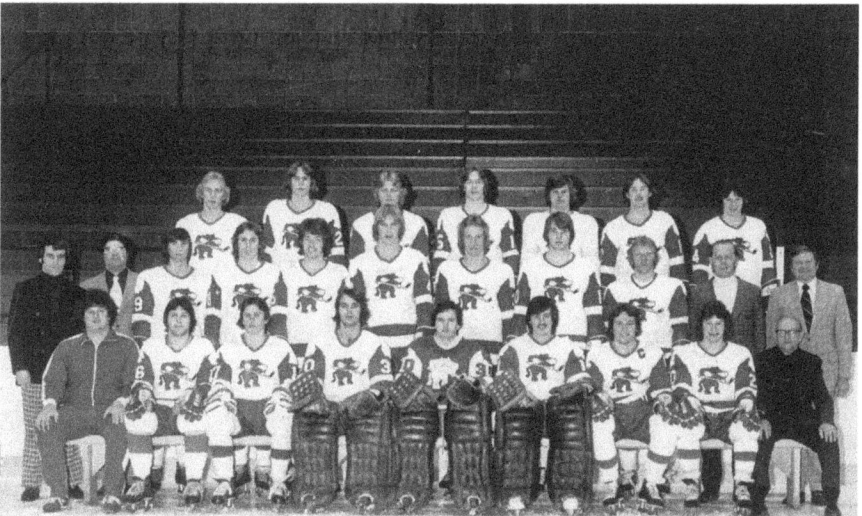

Lou (*second row, second from left*) with the 1976 Austin Mavericks. *USA Hockey*

Vladislav Tretiak getting ready to make a save. *Courtesy of Alexey Tarasov, A. V. Tarasov's grandson*

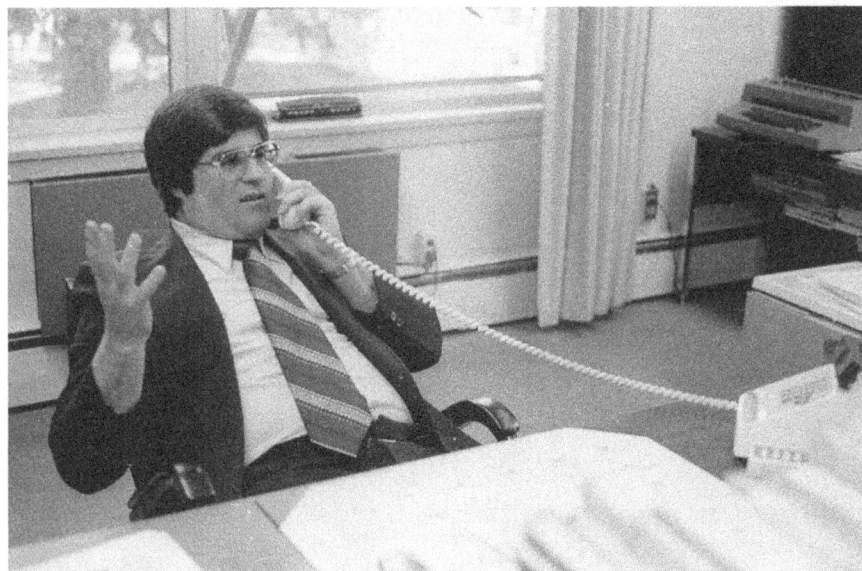

Lou in his office at the Amateur Hockey Association of the United States (AHAUS) in Colorado Springs. *USA Hockey*

Lou and Joni get married in Hawaii. *Collection of the author*

Lou (*standing, far right*) with Tarasov (*standing, second from left*). *Collection of the author*

Vladislav Tretiak and Anatoli Tarasov. *Courtesy of Alexey Tarasov, A. V. Tarasov's grandson*

Lou's sons Brian and Greg.
Collection of the author

Lou coaching at the 1984 Olympics, with Doug Woog. *USA Hockey*

Lou with 1984 Olympic team stars, clockwise from top: Al Iafrate, David A. Jensen, Ed Olczyk, Pat LaFontaine. *USA Hockey*

Lou's son Greg.
Collection of the author

Lou's New Jersey Devils card. *Collection of the author*

Lou with assistant coaches in 2002, Mark Johnson (*left*) and Dean Blais (*right*). *USA Hockey*

Lou at US Hockey Hall of Fame, 2008. *USA Hockey*

Lou with Willie O'Ree, 2014. *USA Hockey*

Lou's great friend Yuri Karmanov. *Collection of the author*

Lou coaching at the 1984 Olympics, with Doug Woog. *USA Hockey*

Lou with 1984 Olympic team stars, clockwise from top: Al Iafrate, David A. Jensen, Ed Olczyk, Pat LaFontaine. *USA Hockey*

Lou's son Greg.
Collection of the author

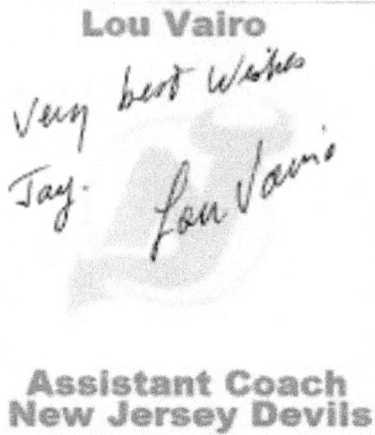

Lou's New Jersey Devils card. *Collection of the author*

Lou with assistant coaches in 2002, Mark Johnson (*left*) and Dean Blais (*right*). *USA Hockey*

Lou at US Hockey Hall of Fame, 2008. *USA Hockey*

Lou with Willie O'Ree, 2014. *USA Hockey*

Lou's great friend Yuri Karmanov. *Collection of the author*

CHAPTER 8

The Next Miracle?

WHEN I COACHED THE US OLYMPIC HOCKEY TEAM IN 1984, I DID NOT apply for that job. Bob Johnson wanted me to come to Calgary to work with him as an assistant with the Calgary Flames, as he was the head coach.

There were a few factors that made it attractive. Firstly, my wife liked Bob Johnson's wife, Martha, and Calgary was a short plane ride from Colorado Springs where my wife was from, so she could get home and see her family when I was away working.

In fact, my wife and I met through hockey. I was working at AHAUS, and I asked if I could possibly have a secretary. I hadn't had one ever before. I mean, I didn't need one when I was installing air conditioners, but now at AHAUS I had paperwork to deal with and I could use a little help. AHAUS didn't have the money to pay for one exclusively for me. So I would have to share the secretary with someone else. I said fine. I didn't need a full-time secretary. I just needed an extra pair of hands, now and then.

I didn't even do the interview with her, but Joni Brown got hired and I had a secretary. She also happened to be very attractive, blonde, and fit, which was a nice bonus. She was a very sweet person, polite and soft-spoken, and easy to work with. She showed up on time, and she always finished whatever I needed done. She was excellent.

There were no romantic thoughts about her on my part. I was about thirteen years older than she was, and I was seeing, on and off, two other women at the time. So there was zero interest on my part other than to

89

notice that Joni was young and pretty. She worked with me. And she was already in a relationship.

As coworkers, she would sometimes mention her relationship to me, and I would mention mine to her. I could see that she was having a hard time in her relationship, but I didn't want to pry. She could tell me what she wanted to tell me.

After Joni had been at AHAUS for over a year, I realized that I had developed a little interest in her, but I was still seeing one of those other women. I wanted to ask Joni out, but not to lunch because that would be somewhere close to the office, and it would look suspect for us to be hatching a plot over lunch, perhaps.

So I asked Joni if she wanted to have dinner with me. I told her that I was going to such a restaurant far from AHAUS and asked if she would care to join me. And she said, "Yes, that would be great! Thank you so much." And that's really how we began.

When we became more serious, I went and spoke to my boss, Hal Trumble, and told him that Joni and I had been dating and that we "kind of liked" each other. I lowballed it, to be sure, because I did not want either of us to lose our jobs. I told him that I did not know where it was going to lead, but I wanted to know if it would be a problem for him, and for the organization.

Hal said, "No, not at all. Excellent choice, Lou, she's a lovely young lady."

Before you knew it, things heated up, and in a year, or two, Joni had moved in with me, into a house I had up in the mountains of Colorado Springs. But before Joni moved in, I asked for a meeting with her parents, because I am old-fashioned.

I told her mother and father what was up. "I'm thirteen years older than Joni," I said. "I don't know how you feel about our relationship. But we're fairly serious. And we'd like to live together to see if it's going to work out, or not. But we're not going to do it without your permission. We wouldn't do that."

Joni's mother, Winona, was very nervous about it. She said, "We sure like you very much, Lou. But I am a mom and in the church, and it makes it very awkward for me." I guessed that Joni moving in with an Italian Catholic from Brooklyn would not go down well at her church.

Her dad, Charlie, scratched his head. He was an old Texas rancher and he said, "Well, first of all, we really appreciate that you would ask our opinion. You don't need our permission, but the fact that you asked us makes us see that you were brought up right."

After taking this in, her mother then changed her tone, and said to me, "Well, you're gonna do it, no matter what we say. Go for it. We trust God. We know Joni's a good gal. And we like you."

So Joni moved in. My family was mortified by my living arrangements in Colorado. I had one grandmother living, and we had always been very close. She couldn't stand the fact that we weren't married, and yet we were living together. It grated against her Italian Catholic soul, and she just thought it was awful. And she laid the blame for it all on me, one hundred percent.

Before we were married, we went to visit her in Brooklyn. Joni was a lady, and she didn't want to embarrass herself, and I didn't want her to feel embarrassed. But my grandmother very quickly took care of any potential cause for embarrassment.

My grandmother pointed her crooked finger at me the way she had done when she was angry with me, ever since I was a little kid, and she said, "You sleep here on the couch. Joni, I have another bed in my room. You're going to sleep with me in my room and we have separate beds."

And that was it. There was no discussion. You had to be respectful. And Joni was respectful. So that's what we did.

We lived together, we grew deeper in love, and we got married. But we didn't tell anybody that we were going to tie the knot. I was coaching in the World Championships in 1983 in Japan and I made my pitch to Joni. "Why don't you come with me, and on the way back, we'll stop in Hawaii for a week, and we'll get married?"

She thought that this plan sounded perfect. I told her that there would be nobody there but us. "It's our marriage and it doesn't belong to anybody else anyway."

We did not sleep in separate beds as we had done in Brooklyn when we stopped in Hawaii on our way back from Japan. We bought

Joni a nice wedding dress and we got married barefoot, on the beach in Lahaina, Maui.

It was a beautiful place, with palm trees surrounding us and the smell of paradise wafting in on the Pacific breeze. We got married at sunset. We hired a photographer who was also the minister, and his girlfriend was the witness. And when I put the ring on Joni's finger, people had come out onto the balcony of the Marriott hotel overlooking the beach, and had watched the wedding below, and they all applauded. We took a bow.

We went on a midnight cruise in Lahaina harbor, and toasted our marriage with champagne and feasted on lobster and filet mignon and marveled at the humpback whales which were breaching out of the water. It was romantic. And I was now a married man.

Joni's parents hosted a reception later on when we got back home, which was also very nice. By getting married under the family radar, we had saved a lot of money. So we asked people who wanted to give us wedding gifts to keep it simple, and so, to keep it cash. We were going to put whatever we got into the next house we would buy. People were generous, and that's what we did.

And then Bob Johnson wanted me to come and be an assistant in Calgary. He added that Cliff Fletcher, the GM, had already started the paperwork with the Canadian government so that the guy from Brooklyn would be allowed into the birthplace of hockey to work behind the bench of the Flames.

I was excited at the prospect. However, when Bob asked me to come north, AHAUS was also in the middle of the hunt for a coach for the 1984 Olympic hockey team. And we were not putting the puck in the net.

We had asked six coaches to take the Olympic team helm, and they all had a reason not to do it. One said that it would interfere with his job commitment at the college where he coached. One coach said he didn't want to miss Christmas with his wife and kids. They all had reasons to say no. Most of them didn't want to endure the professional stress that would be loaded on them after the 1980 "Miracle on Ice" gold medal.

And so, when Bob asked me to come to Calgary, we were getting nervous. I didn't think I was ready to take something like assistant coaching on. Coaching wasn't my goal in life. I didn't wake up one day and say, I want to be a coach. It was all accidental. I got out of the army, and a midget coach did not show up, so Bart Grillo asked me to step in. And I got behind the bench—rather, I stood in the stairwell of the rink in Flushing, Queens—and I began my hockey coaching career, never imagining in that vast and dark rink that one day, I would be invited to help coach in the NHL.

After striking out with half a dozen coaches, the AHAUS management came to me. William Thayer Tutt was still the president of AHAUS, and he was a fine man. He and Art Berglund, a veteran hockey guy, and Ron De Gregorio, who was elected to AHAUS board of directors in 1975, came to me and said, "Lou, you know the players. You were there in '80 with Herb. You know the kids coming up because you coached the under-20 junior national team." And then they came to the real and rather desperate point. "We can't get anybody else."

Then suddenly, out of the blue, this other coach said that he would like to coach the Olympic team, and he was a good guy whom I supported, but then, just as suddenly, he changed his mind. He came to me and said, "I'd much rather be your assistant. I'll come as your assistant if you do it." So I told him that we should both interview for the job and let them pick the best coach for it.

In the meantime, my wife, Joni, was annoyed with me because she liked the idea of living in Calgary, and she liked even more the idea that I'd make an NHL kind of salary. AHAUS promised that if I took the Olympic coaching job, that I could have my AHAUS job back after the games were done.

I said no. I was not going to have them bring in someone for a couple of months to do my AHAUS job and then have them lose that job so I could come back to it. That wasn't right.

They agreed and told me that I could bring in whomever I wanted, and I could work out the details with them. I had wide experience in the hockey world, and I knew who was good. And so I did. There was a guy named Keith Blase who I thought would be great. He was in St. Louis, and there was no way I was going to make him "temporarily" move with his family to Colorado Springs.

I told them to bring in Keith, who I knew to be a skilled administrator, and let him loose. I said that once I was gone, I was gone. I had spent five years at AHAUS, and I thought I had done a good job. I had pointed the ship in the right direction, and now another skipper could sail my part of the course. Keith got the job, and he fit right in. And I left to coach the 1984 Olympic hockey team.

I knew that when I left AHAUS to coach the Olympic team I had begun another journey which would lead me to a new place. I thought I would do a good job with the team, because I was going to pick good people to help me.

Tim Taylor was the guy who coached at Yale who wanted to be my assistant, and so he was. Doug Woog, a good coach I knew from my time coaching the Mavericks in Austin, Minnesota, was another, as I had played against his teams many times and saw his talent. Bob O'Connor was another good Minnesota hockey coach who could think outside of the box, and Dave Peterson was a Minnesota goalie who was the director of player development and coaching at AHAUS and wrote goalie coaching manuals. He would be our goalie coach.

I wanted to bring in these guys because they were the best, and I trusted and liked them. I also knew that they were in no way yes men. If I did something which they thought was wrong, they would disagree with me and be unafraid to do that, and we very much needed that kind of environment to put the best team on the ice. I knew that I didn't know everything. I also knew that I would learn. So that's what I put together. A team who would work with me, and from whom I could learn.

I called Bob Johnson and told him that I would not be in Calgary, and he was disappointed. Later he would ask me to come and coach with him in Pittsburgh, when he headed up the Penguins, but I was in Europe and under a contract I will tell you about later.

I wanted to know the players we had available, so I sat down with Art Berglund who had been the manager of the US National Team from 1973 to 1975, and in 1976, he was the general manager of the US Olympic ice hockey team. He would manage it again, and also win the prestigious Lester Patrick Award for his contribution to hockey in 1992.

I had worked with Art for a few years and knew how knowledgeable he was. I wanted to make a depth chart, so we set to work in 1982 to create the 1984 team. He presented me with some goalies, who he hoped would still be available.

I told him we'd probably take two goalies. We were looking at John Vanbiesbrouck and Tom Barrasso. We were also looking at Mike Richter and John Casey. They were all pretty good goalies. However, the two goalies we ended up with, Mark Behrend and Bob Mason, played at a high level.

Behrend grew up in Madison, Wisconsin, and played for the University of Wisconsin Badgers, where he was the MVP in the 1981 and 1983 NCAA tournaments, both of which Wisconsin won. Mason was a Minnesota guy, from International Falls, and at the University of Minnesota Duluth.

They played very well in the pre-Olympic trial, and they also played extremely well in the games themselves. We were very solid in goal, but I want you to know that we weren't able to secure the goalies that we rated ahead of the ones we did have. I don't think that we would have won a gold medal without Jimmy Craig in 1980, but all that you can really deal with is who is available. And we took the best we could.

In many ways, we were constrained by our success in 1980. I looked at defensemen, many of whom I had coached. There was Greg Ludwig and Phil Housley, and many other great young d-men, but they had all signed with NHL teams. The NHL general managers looked at our success at Lake Placid and said, "Hmm, these American kids can play hockey. We had better sign them fast." And so they did, which took them off our Olympic players list.

I looked at what forwards were available. I started at center ice and saw that there was a young phenom playing in the Quebec League who was breaking all of *le grande* Guy Lafleur's records. A kid named Pat LaFontaine, who was seventeen years old in 1982. I thought he should be one of our centermen and Art Berglund said, "Yeah, great, but you also have Bobby Carpenter and Aaron Broten." It turned out that I did not. They had signed with the NHL. But I did manage to get Pat LaFontaine.

It was the same with the wingers. Brian Mullen was top of my list, but he and many other fine young wingers all signed with the pros. They didn't want to wait two years for their shot at the NHL, and I didn't blame them.

I was never mad at them—except for the goalie, Tom Barrasso. He was about seventeen years old when I first had him on that pre-Olympic team. He worked out in July 1982 at the Air Force Academy training on and off the ice in Colorado Springs, and he went to Finland with us, where we played some exhibition games.

We also went to Alaska, where we played four games against the Soviet Wings, and Barrasso played excellently in one game. A guy came up to me before that game, and he said, "Can I introduce myself? My name is Seymour Knox." He was the owner and president of the Buffalo Sabres, and he had the elegant, patrician look to him as would a guy who was the grandson of the founder of Woolworths. "Tommy Barrasso is a draft pick of ours. And I want to know if it's possible, Lou, without upsetting your plan, or your schedule, if there is any way I can get to say hello to Tommy?"

He was very polite and congenial, and I said, "Sure. It's a pleasure to meet you. You've come all this way from Buffalo to meet him, of course you can say hello."

Knox then felt compelled to tell me that he had a private plane in which he flew up to Alaska. Just in case I had mistaken him for the hoi polloi. "I want to see Tommy play," he said. "And I'd love to meet him. I'd love to sit and talk with him."

I should have already smelled a rat, but I did not. I said, "We have a meal after the game. And you're invited."

I put Seymour Knox III at a private table with Tom Barrasso. I was trying to be a good host in welcoming all the hockey world to the table, as it were. The meal ended and everybody got on the bus back to Anchorage, where we played another game against the Soviet Wings. Tom played another good game, which ended in a tie. The Soviet Wings played exhibition games against the NHL teams, so it wasn't like we were playing a beer league squad. They were good.

Then I got a call at six o'clock the next morning from Larry Johnson, who was our team manager. Larry said, "Lou, we have a problem. Barrasso is gone." I asked where he went. He said, "Seymour Knox's agent just called me from Toronto and Seymour Knox flew off with him on his private jet and they're signing him today." Barrasso had turned pro and was gone. It didn't matter, as I didn't want him anymore, because he didn't want us.

However, I was extremely disappointed and hurt that it was done the way it was done. All Tom had to do was come and say to me: "Coach, this is just not for me. I need to go." And believe me, I wouldn't have attempted to keep him with us if he wasn't happy. I've never believed in refusing to release a player who wants to go. I think it's terrible in youth hockey that kids get tied up to places and teams. They should be able to go wherever they want to play. It should be what's best for the player.

I said to Larry, "Mr. Seymour Knox could have told me what was up. Did he say anything to you?" Larry said no, he never said a word. And we treated them graciously. So off Barrasso went to Buffalo, and we continued on.

Our exhibition game play was superb. We had nine players under the age of twenty on our team in those games. Pat LaFontaine, Al Iafrate, Ed Olcyk, and Chris Chelios, who just turned twenty in 1982. People need to know how hard those kids worked and how truly wonderful they were.

We beat a lot of teams, some of them in the NHL. We beat the undefeated Washington Capitals 2–1. They were undefeated. They had eight wins and no losses in preseason games. It was wonderful. We played the Minnesota North Stars and beat them; we tied the Detroit Red Wings at home. We even beat the New York Rangers, and Herb Brooks was their coach, in Lake Placid.

I saw Craig Patrick before the game. I asked if he and Herb would come down and say hello to the team. I said, "You guys were the legends of this event, winning it all in 1980." I told Craig that I had left a message for Herb but that he had not responded to me. In fact, anytime I had asked him to come and help evaluate the players, he didn't want to do it. He said that 1980 was then, and this was now. "It's your thing now, so you do it," was his response.

I felt bad because I helped him when he asked. I tried my best for him. And I really wanted him to come and say hello to my team. He wouldn't do it.

I felt hurt. I knew how inspiring it would have been to bring him into the team dressing room and let the kids shake his hand and hear his wisdom. He didn't even coach behind the bench the night we played the Rangers. He had his assistant coach the team. Herb sat upstairs, in the press box.

When the game was over, I went to see him just to say hello to him. He was walking fast, and he ignored me when I called him. He hustled to the Rangers bus and got on it. And disappeared.

Herb was very close friends with our team manager, Larry Johnson. They were former teammates. And Larry was with me. Larry shook his head and said, "That's Herb. Let him go. Don't chase him, Lou." So I let him go.

I'm not saying that to make him look bad. I still love him and respect him and think he's an American sports hero. That's just the way he was, and what people said when he exhibited behavior they found puzzling: "Herbie is Herbie."

Our game against the Rangers was only an exhibition game but my team had beaten the team of my boyhood, so I had more than a little bit of a thrill at that. But I wasn't thinking that a win guaranteed us anything at the Olympics. And I will tell you a funny story about that night against the Rangers.

The famous linesman John D'Amico was working in front of our bench, as that was his side of the ice. Now I had learned from Fred Shero that the only thing that you ever say to referees or linesmen during a game is "Good evening," at the beginning and "Good night, and thank you," after the game. This was what Fred taught me and it is a creed I live still today.

So I'm behind our bench, looking right out on the blue line. The Rangers Anders Hedberg and Mark Pavelich were coming into our zone in a two on one. And Hedberg was offside by about a half a foot. John D'Amico was right there on the line, but he didn't call Hedberg offside. I didn't say anything to the linesman. I just said to myself, "Offside."

John D'Amico jumped up on the boards in front of me and turned to look at me. Then he said, "That's enough outta you, college boy."

Most Olympic coaches were college coaches first. So I said, "Who are you talking about, John? I didn't even go to college."

He took that information in, then he said, "I might have missed that one."

And then, to make up for his miss, he added, "You got the same dummy out there taking face-offs. He's been beaten twice now in the first period in your own end." I asked him who it was, and he told me. "Thanks for the tip, John," I said, and he skated off.

The next face-off that we had in our end, I pulled that centerman who had been beaten and put out a different one who won the face-off. And John turned and smiled at me. We were even.

Our preparation for the Olympics was thrilling. We not only played NHL teams and the Soviets in our sixty-five-game pre-Olympic schedule, but we also played the United States' second national hockey team, the B team, in a series. We beat them in Lake Placid, and they beat us. We came back and played a great game in Cleveland and beat them again, and then we had a four all tie in Cincinnati. It was excellent hockey. And they had some really good players on the second national team. It was a good test for us. And our kids responded. I knew they would give it their all in the Olympic games.

Ours was the youngest US hockey team ever assembled in an Olympic year, with the average age being about twenty. Two players from the 1980s team came back—John Harrington and Phil Verchota—and we had three players with one year of high school remaining—David A. Jensen (we also had David H. Jensen, who was twenty-two), Al Iafrate, and Ed Olczyk. We had seven players from Boston and nine from Minnesota.

At the end of September 1983, with the Olympics kicking off in five months, we were hosted at the White House by Ronald Reagan. The president shook hands with all the players, and our forward and captain Phil Verchota gave Ronald Reagan his own red, white, and blue Olympic jersey. I couldn't hear what Verchota said to Reagan when he handed over the jersey, but the president smiled and then joked, "Just got an offer to play tomorrow night."

Ronald Reagan came up to me and he said, "You must be Lou Vairo, the coach. I am honored to meet you." And he put his hand out with a big smile. And I put out mine, and then I stopped. And I took my watch off and put it safely in my pocket. Then I shook his hand, and he looked at me as if stunned. He said, "What the hell is that about?" I said to him, "Oh, I know you politicians like shiny things," and he couldn't stop laughing. He thought it was the funniest thing ever to share with his wife and Vice President George H. W. Bush and his wife, and they were all laughing. It was a nice night.

I also got the keys to the City of New York from Mayor Ed Koch. We were getting ready to take the team to Europe, and we had been practicing on Long Island. About 6,000 people showed up to cheer us on. It was beautiful.

They had a ceremony for me at City Hall, and when the mayor gave me the keys, I asked him "Are these the keys to the vault?"

He looked and me and said, "If we had anything in the vault, do you think I'd be giving you the damn keys?"

We had a good laugh at that.

There were some things that happened on our 1984 Olympic journey that were not funny, and that no one knows about, and which I never talked about publicly during the Olympics, or later. They all put our team at a disadvantage.

Alan Eagleson, the Canadian lawyer and player agent who was the brains behind the Canada Cup, an international ice hockey tournament that was invitation only, was involved in one of them.

Now, I like Alan Eagleson. I know he went to jail for the bad things he had done to hockey players, but I like him. He also did a lot of positive things for hockey, such as organizing the historic 1972 Canada-Soviet Summit Series that changed hockey.

In fact, Alan Eagleson once did me a personal service that was most unexpected. He carried my luggage to my hotel room. He was in the lobby of a hotel that I was checking into in Sweden, and he saw me and saw that I was exhausted, so he came up and said, "Oh my, you must be exhausted after your long trip, sir, let me carry your bags!"

So he carried my luggage to my room. I gave him a US quarter as a tip. And he clutched it in his fist as if it were gold. We laughed and I gave him a hug and a pat on the back.

But this was before the political dealing he did which harmed my Olympic team.

At the time, a player could not sign any kind of professional contract and still be eligible for international play and certainly not for the Olympic games.

The New York Islanders had drafted Pat LaFontaine, but they were very supportive of his Olympic goals. I want to highly commend Al Arbor, and the GM, Bill Torre, and Pat's agent, Don Meehan. It was a pleasure to work with them. They came to me and said that Pat wanted to play in the Olympics, and they wanted him to play in the Olympics. They were upfront and straightforward. Everything they did was class. They would not sign Pat until after the Olympics, and they wanted me to know that and not to worry about it. Ours was a wonderful relationship.

Our team was supposed to go to Germany for our pre-Olympic tour before we went to the Games in Sarajevo, and we were to play Germany two or three times. The Germans were a good opponent, and they would have been a real test for us. At the last minute, our games were canceled and were instead given to Team Canada. They had replaced us.

We had to scramble, and we finally got Austria to agree to play us. But it wasn't the same. They treated us very hospitably, but the Austrian team was not at the same level of competition as the Germans were. It hurt us. And then I found out what happened.

Alan Eagleson had gone to see Roman Neumayer, who was the head of the German Ice Hockey Federation. He was a good guy and a friend of mine. I love Roman. But he did a bad thing. Eagleson made a deal with him. If Germany played Team Canada, Eagleson would invite them to the Canada Cup. And so they did, and so they were invited to the Canada Cup in September of 1984. After the Olympics.

It got worse. On the morning of our game against Canada in the Olympics, Thayer Tutt, the president of AHAUS, came to see me. He was the nicest man you'll ever meet in your life. He said, "Lou, I need you to cooperate on this. And I hope you don't get mad at me. But it's been done." I asked him "What has been done?"

He told me that the Canadian team forward Dave Gagner and about three or four Canadian players who were pretty fine were not supposed to play in the Olympics because they had signed NHL contracts. Some had even received bonus money, which made them ineligible. But they were going to play against us. Thayer had agreed to it.

If we would have known that the rule was going to be changed four hours before our first game with Canada, in the Olympics, we would have agreed with Canada to fix it six or seven months earlier. We would have said, "Let's get that rule changed. And we'll both do it."

We had players like Ron Wilson who wanted to play, and Dave Delich. They were really good players. There were senior age players playing pro in the minors or in Europe who we could have used. We wanted Craig Norwich, who was at the University of Wisconsin and became the second defenseman in NCAA history to lead his team in scoring and win the NCAA Championship in the same season. He was playing pro. We might have won the gold medal with those guys. We couldn't use them because we followed the IIHF rules, which barred players from playing for us if they were pro.

So now we were going to play against Canada, and their pros, in the first game in Sarajevo. I don't know what the exact trade-offs were. Maybe Thayer was told by Eagleson that he could have one of the Canada Cup games in Madison Square Garden and keep the gate receipts or something for AHAUS. I don't know what benefited AHAUS to do it financially and can only guess. I did know that I was stunned.

That dire revelation came on top of other bad news. Bud Kessel, our fifty-six-year-old equipment manager, had a heart attack in his room that morning and had to be rushed to the hospital. He survived, thank goodness.

Then the team doctor, Dr. George Nagobads, who had just been appointed our chief medical officer, came to me to tell me that he would not allow me to play Pat LaFontaine, who was our best player.

"I forbid you to play him, Lou. He is very sick. He has asthma and other things. I can't give him the medicine that can take care of it because it's against the doping rules, and we would forfeit. He has a fever, and he can't play." This was a few hours before our game.

I went into the Olympic Village and found Pat's parents. His father said that they would sign any waiver I wanted them to sign so Pat could play. "He had not signed with the Islanders in order to play in the Olympics," his father said. "He's had asthma his whole life, and he's played hockey with it. He's not going to die if he plays, but he's not going to be a hundred percent. But he can play."

I then went and spoke to Pat and asked him how he felt. He told me that he really wanted to play, so I made a decision. I went back to see Dr. Nagobads, who was twenty-five years older than me and who I loved as a father. But I said, "Doc, I treasure and respect everything you say and do but you're not the coach, I am. I'm responsible for the team. And I have to have final say. If the player doesn't want to play, that's another story. Pat says he can play and wants to play so he's going to play."

The doctor, who was from Latvia and had studied in Germany, was furious. "You do what you want to do!" he shouted at me, then stomped out of the room. He refused to speak to me for about a year after that, as well.

And a few of our players had food poisoning. Our players would follow the Italian team players when they ate, as the Italians had their own chefs and food, and then our guys would devour whatever the Italians left behind. We were in rough shape.

Our first game was against Canada, and it was an afternoon game, scheduled to start at 1:30 p.m. inside the Zetra Arena, which was a brand-new rink in the center of Sarajevo. We left our residence three and a half hours before the game started so the guys would have time to prepare physically and mentally for this first big test.

That plan fell apart fast. We got on the bus, and right away, I could tell that our driver was drunk. I could smell it, and I could see it in his driving. He made wrong turns, and then, when he finally found his way, we wound up in crazy traffic, which was due to the fact we were now behind the guy who was running the torch which would light the flame to start the Games the next day. Yes, we were playing a day before the

Games officially opened. And now we were stuck behind the Olympic torch.

By the time we got to the arena, it was 12:55. The game was going to start in 35 minutes, and Canada was already on the ice, warming up. So much for our extra time to prepare. The guys got dressed fast and then they were on the ice, but it had been a disaster that was only going to get worse.

Team Canada's first shot of the game, taken by Pat Flatley, hit Chris Chelios in the foot. Chelios wound up with two broken bones. So here are my two best players, LaFontaine and Chelios, not able to play their best, or at all. I saw Chelios limping along in the corridor, and I said, "I'm really sorry, Chris, but you're out."

He said, "I'm not out. They're going to give me a walking cast. They will tape it up, and I can play." That's Chris Chelios. He played the entire Olympics with two broken bones in his foot.

And so with those two players not at one hundred percent, I upgraded David A. Jensen. He was my third best talent. But he hadn't skated for three weeks because in our final exhibition game against Canada, he got a knee injury.

We had a knee brace made for him, but it got lost on its way to Yugoslavia. Finally it arrived and Jensen skated with it. He said it didn't fit completely right, but he played with his knee in a brace. He was on the "Diaper Line" with Pat LaFontaine and Eddie Olczyk, called that because they were all so young.

We lost our opening game 4–2, and it was one that we needed to win to have a shot. Now we had one day to get ourselves back together before we played the Czechs. They were even better than the Canadians, and we had to beat them if we had any hope of getting out of Group B and into the medal round.

The Czechs were a tough, fast team, and they also had motivation to beat us, as it was the US team in 1980 that had thrashed them 7–3. In their first game against Norway, they had put sixty-six shots on goal, and ten of those shots went in. The Norwegians scored four goals in their 10–4 defeat, so we knew that the Czechs weren't impregnable. They were just very good.

We went down a goal in the first, and then the arena's lights went out and we were in the dark. The game was delayed for about half an hour, but it was a sign of things to come. Our lights went out, too. We tied the score, but then did ourselves in with bad penalties. The Czechs got two power play goals and beat us 4–1. We all knew that we were not going to win a gold medal now.

We tied Norway 3–3, beat Austria 7–3, then tied Finland 3–3, and beat Poland 7–4. And that was it. We finished in seventh place, and our Olympic Games were done.

The world doesn't know how good that 1984 team really was. But our three top players were not even close to playing in full health. The biggest disappointment to me is how good these kids were, how hard they worked for a whole year before the Games. They put everything they had into their game, but it was not enough. There would be no miracle on ice this time.

I had a lot of soul searching to do myself after we failed to win anything in 1984 at the Olympic Games. There were things I could have done better, and differently, and hindsight is perfect for that. At the time I tried to do my best with the team we had, and they did, too. It's the beauty and the sadness of sport. You never know who is going to win until the final buzzer sounds.

Now that the Games were over, and my job was filled by a very good guy at AHAUS, I had to think about what I would do next. I had no idea, in February of 1984, that pretty soon I would be following all those players I could not get for our Olympic team to the NHL myself.

CHAPTER 9

The Big Time

AFTER THE 1984 OLYMPICS I WAS PRETTY DICOURAGED. I WAS PLAYING the Games over and over in my head, and I still couldn't change the result. We finished with a record of two wins, two ties, and two losses. We didn't qualify for the medal round, and we had a lot of injuries. I loved the team, but I had just spent some of the worst days of my life in hockey. And I had to stand up and take a beating from the media, who all expected another miracle. I still take a beating. And so be it.

I had then, and still have today, just one regret. That's the fact the world did not know how good that team was. Those young players, many still teenagers, worked their asses off from the minute they were selected until the end of the Olympics. They really did. They were great guys and very talented.

But everything just caught up to us all at once. Whenever anyone says "injuries are no excuse" I get very annoyed. It's a stupid thing to say injuries don't matter because of course they do. If you lose your best players, it matters. But I was just upset that the world never saw our true team and what a good team it really was. And I'll take that to my grave.

So after the Olympics I was back home in Colorado Springs, trying to figure out what I would do next. I was thinking about getting into the restaurant business. I love to cook, and love food, and thought the restaurant world would be a completely different world than hockey. I also thought that maybe I needed that kind of change.

My wife, Joni, agreed. She thought opening a restaurant was a fine idea. Especially since she was five months pregnant with our first child.

After the 1984 Olympics, I was thinking that I was probably a better cook than I was a coach. I had grown up with Italian cuisine as our household specialty, had worked in an Italian restaurant in college, and had run a kitchen in the army. The restaurant business was something I knew. Even the fifteen-hour days, six days a week, appealed to me. I would at least be at home with Joni and the baby.

About three months after the Games were over, I received a call from the New Jersey Devils general manager, Max McNab. He said, "Well, we're thinking of making some coaching changes, and we'd like to talk to you. Would you be willing to fly into New Jersey to meet with our owners John McMullen and John Whitehead?"

I said that I would. I knew a bit about the New Jersey Devils because before they moved to New Jersey in 1982 they had been the Colorado Rockies. I had scouted for a number of years for the Colorado Rockies when I was working for USA Hockey. The GM of the Rockies, Ray Miron, approached me out of the blue at a Colorado Rockies hockey game at McNichols arena. He said, "You've coached in the world juniors. You get around and see all these players in Europe and America. Why don't you scout for us?"

So I did. I had been in the room with some very good scouts. I knew Bob Davidson, the former captain of the Stanley Cup champion Toronto Maple Leafs, one of the nicest men I've ever met, and he had scouted for the Leafs. There was Frank Mario, a former NHLer with Boston, and Aldo Guidolin, who played for the Rangers and became the director of player development for the Rockies. They were all good guys. But they didn't know anything at all about American college kids or about European players.

When I was in meetings with them, I would stay quiet. I loved listening to them and hearing their opinions on players. Eventually, they would come around to me and ask, "Lou? You have anybody you like?" "I sure do," I said. "Guys I coach. Or coached against. I like Aaron Broten at the University of Minnesota and I had him on the world junior team. His brother Neal is a top-notch player, too, drafted by the North Stars. And I like the young defenseman at Wisconsin, Bruce Driver."

They drafted all of those players in later rounds of the NHL draft, and they turned out to be terrific NHL players. But when I would mention the Swedish goaling sensation Pelle Lindbergh, or the wonderful Mats Naslund and Tomas Eriksson and Tomas Jonnson, they didn't know who they were. I knew how good these guys were, but it wasn't always easy to convey that.

Here's what I was up against. A proven NHL commodity were the players who excelled in major junior hockey, especially in the Ontario Hockey League, the Quebec league, and the western Canadian league. In the entire history of the NHL, that's where the overwhelming majority of the players came from.

Players who had their sights set on the NHL would play junior hockey in the Canadian junior leagues. And it was the odd American college player that would get selected here and there to play in the world's premier hockey league. Europeans, however, weren't even on the radar yet.

I had some NHL scouting experience when I flew to New Jersey to meet with John McMullen and John Whitehead. McMullen had a master's degree in naval architecture and engineering from the Massachusetts Institute of Technology and a doctorate in mechanical engineering from the Swiss Federal Institute of Technology in Zürich. Whitehead had an MBA from Harvard and was cochairman and co-senior partner at Goldman Sachs. I knew that I wasn't going to impress these guys by being anything other than myself.

People would say to me, "Make sure you're on your best behavior!" I thought, I will just be myself, because I can't fake that. So I was relaxed with these two tycoons, and as a result, they were relaxed with me, in a yin and yang kind of way.

Mr. Whitehead, who was then in his early sixties, was showing me all the photographs on his wall of him with the Shah of Iran and a collection of presidents and political figures, as he knew everyone from his position at Goldman, and he had also served as the deputy secretary of state under President Reagan. So that's how he let me know who he was.

Dr. McMullen could not have been more down-to-earth. He was then in his late sixties, but you could still see the Irish kid from Jersey City in him. He had been a navy man, having graduated from the US

Naval Academy in 1940, just in time to serve in World War II. He became a commander, and then from there went on to own a shipping business, and part of the New York Yankees, and the Houston Astros. In 1982, he made a bid for the Colorado Rockies and moved them east, "close enough" to my old stomping grounds.

Anyway, John McMullen turned out to be just a wonderful man, who was a devoted sports guy. He knew I was a Yankees fan, and he joked that if I ever wanted to look up the true meaning of a minority owner, "You'll find a picture of anybody, like me, who has ever been one with George Steinbrenner. . . ." It was funny, as McMullen was a minority owner of the Yankees, and Steinbrenner was the team's famously intense majority owner, who brooked no opposition.

John McMullen and John Whitehead took me to dinner with the president of the team, Bob Butera, who ran for governor of Pennsylvania once and almost won. Also, there was Max McNab, the general manager of the Devils. Again, two really fine guys. We had a nice night, as I told them about my hockey life, and they listened.

Then I was invited to meet with Dr. McMullen and Max McNab and Bob Butera in McMullen's office on the twenty-second floor of the World Trade Center. McMullen rolled up the sleeves of his white shirt, as it was summertime. And he said, "Let's talk."

Then he did. He told me that he admired my work in hockey, and he saw the dividends that were going to pay off for players who had worked with me. Then he raised the level of the conversation and said, "We're looking for a head coach and an assistant coach. We're also looking for a head coach-slash-general manager, in Portland, Maine, in our minor league system. And we think you can fit into any four of those categories. How do you feel about it?"

I was flattered to be considered for any of those jobs, and then I told him the truth. "I have coached some good teams, and against some good teams," I said. "And we've had success, but I don't know the NHL like I need to know it to be a successful head coach. I don't think the players would accept my background. I think you'd be taking a risk by making me head coach of the Devils. I'd like to learn more about the league."

They all listened as I went on, as I wasn't trying to convince them not to hire me. Just to hire me for the right job. "If I can choose between all four positions," I continued, "I would be very comfortable as assistant coach with the New Jersey Devils."

Bob Butera thanked me and said that they had some other names they were looking at, and I figured the meeting was over. But then Dr. McMullen, with his sleeves all rolled up, said, "No, no, no, no, no! I want Lou to be part of this organization. I like his character. I like his positive attitude. I think that maybe I was insane when I bought this team with John Whitehead. But I like Lou's positive outlook on it. Reminds me of Tommy Lasorda, who was always upbeat."

I was very happy to be compared to the great baseball player and manager Tommy Lasorda. I had played catch with him when I was a kid in Brooklyn at Ebbets Field, when Lasorda was a pitcher for the Dodgers, and we'd get to play with the team on Saturday mornings. Now he was the very successful manager of the Los Angeles Dodgers.

So I said, "Who would you consider as head coach? Because I want this to succeed. And I don't want you guys to stick your neck out for me. I don't operate like that."

Max McNab said, "Do you know Doug Carpenter?"

I had heard of him. He had coached in New Haven. I told them that if they selected Carpenter as their head coach, he would have to accept me as an assistant. It would have to be his call. "If you offer him that coaching job, you can't say to him, you have to take Lou, that wouldn't be fair to him," I told them. "He has to be able to choose who he wants."

Max said that they were going to talk it all over to see if they decided to go with Doug.

I said, "If you decide to go with Doug, you can tell him you'd like me to come in as assistant coach. But I want to talk to him first, before I make any decision. I want to talk to him." And they agreed.

I met on my own with John McMullen who produced a long contract with print so fine I couldn't read it. He told me that if they hired me as an assistant coach, this is what they would pay me, and so on, for a one-year deal. I said, "Dr. McMullen, a handshake is good enough for me."

I don't think he quite heard me, because he continued, "Well, this is what we're recommending for pay. But we can negotiate."

I said, "I don't care what it is. I'm happy that you want me, and a handshake is good enough and you don't owe me anything if you fire me. I don't want money that I didn't earn."

McMullen looked at me as if he was meeting someone from a lost time and place. He said, "Oh my. If I could get just two players on the Houston Astros to agree to that we wouldn't lose money, we would make money." He was impressed by how I was handling the offer. I told him to fill in the numbers when we finally agreed on the job, but first they needed to speak to Doug Carpenter.

They did, and offered Doug the coaching job, and then told him that they were thinking of me as his assistant, and that I wanted to speak to him. So then I spoke to Doug, and I told him not to feel any pressure. "We don't even know each other," I said, so I didn't expect him to leap at the chance to work with me.

It turns out that he did know me. "When I was in the American League, we had some kids coming from Canada and they couldn't play in the United States until their transfers were sorted out and I couldn't find the person at USA Hockey to do it. And then the receptionist said, 'Let me connect you with Lou Vairo. He may be able to help.'"

I kind of vaguely remembered this but he went on. "I asked if there was any way that I could get these transfers sorted as there was a game that night and I needed those guys in the lineup."

I told him that my colleague who handled transfers was out sick, but that I would get back to him. So I called my colleague Kim Folsom, and she told me that she was not contagious, she just wasn't feeling very good. I asked her if I brought her the transfer cards, could she sign off on them? She said yes, and so I did. I was able to get Doug his players, and he was able to get them in the game.

He said, "I never forgot that, Lou. Not a lot of people would bother to do that. I really appreciated that. And I'd love to have you as my assistant on the Devils." And that's how that happened.

The Devils' brass wanted to go to Little Italy to celebrate with a nice dinner, and that's what we did. McMullen really liked the fact that I had told him a handshake was good enough for me, and while he gave me an actual written contract, he never forgot that. He was wonderful to work for.

I went to the Devils' training camp, which was fascinating. There were the grizzled veterans, like Richie Preston, Mel Bridgman, Bob Lorimer, Don Lever, Ron Low, and Chico Resch. We had young guys like Aaron Broten, Bruce Driver (guys I had wanted for the 1984 Olympic team), Greg Adams, and Pat Verbeek, along with John MacLean who was nineteen years old, and Kirk Muller, who was just eighteen. We had some talented veterans and some rising young stars.

All these guys were so welcoming, and very nice to me. There was no "who is this guy from Brooklyn talking hockey to us NHLers?" attitude. They all knew me as a hockey coach, so that was good. However, it took me a little while to figure out what my role as an assistant was. I was pushing pucks around on the ice at practice, and I broke film down at times, which I wasn't a big fan of doing, as I felt that my time could be better spent watching players and analyzing them in real time. Which is what I did.

I made advanced scouting trips before we played other teams and while we were playing, I sat in the press box and would come down and report on what I had seen after each period. Doug Carpenter wanted me to be on the bench, but I told him that I couldn't see anything from the bench. I told him that if I was sitting up in the press box, I would have a TV in front of me, and I could see the replays and could know exactly what's going on if I missed something. I didn't need to be seen behind the bench on TV close-ups to help the team. Doug was an excellent bench coach. That was his biggest strength, and I let him do it. He didn't need me there. And he let me do my thing.

Doug was forty-two, so a couple of years older than me at the time. He was intense, in a low-key way. He had just led the Cornwall, Ontario, junior team to victory in the Memorial Cup. The great Punch Imlach thought so highly of him that he hired him to coach the Toronto Maple Leafs farm team in Moncton (New Brunswick) for the 1980–1981 season, and then moved him on to Cincinnati in the AHL. He had paid his dues in the minors.

And I was happy to be his assistant. I had no secret desire to be a head coach. I wanted to be supportive to everyone on the team, and to help them to be their best. I knew that no matter how hard I worked, I wasn't facing the same pressure as Doug was, and that was fine with me. I just didn't want to be in that spotlight.

I got a chance to rub shoulders with a guy who had very much enjoyed the spotlight, and whose wit had done much to keep people laughing with the Devils, until, inevitably, they were laughing at them. Tom McVie, who had coached the Devils the year before, which was their worst year so far in terms of wins and losses, wound up coaching the Utica Devils for a couple of years, and then came back in the early 1990s as the Devils' head coach again.

He and I got along very well, and I loved to break his balls. He was running a practice in training camp. When the guys were just warming up and stretching out their legs, he would be doing push-ups. Afterwards, I told him that he was very impressive out on the ice, doing push-ups. He said, "I'm a health nut. I'm into all that. That's called a Tommy McVie practice. You got the next one. What are you going to do?"

So I went to the snack bar, and I got a coffee and a doughnut, and I went out on the ice. I put the coffee and the donut on the boards by the bench and I called the players over. Then I took a bite of the doughnut and a sip of the coffee. I said, "This is a Lou Vairo practice." Tommy McVie laughed and laughed at that.

It was a treat to get to know him. He was an old timer who subscribed to the philosophy of "If you can't beat them in the alley, you can't beat them on the ice." We disagreed about that, but I loved him anyway. We need people like that in the game. They make the game alive.

Another guy I really liked, and learned a lot from, was our general manager, Max McNab. Max had been a forward for the Detroit Red Wings and had won the Stanley Cup with them in 1950. He had been the GM of the Washington Capitals for seven years, from 1975 until 1982, and then midway through the Devils' 1983–1984 season he had come on board as the New Jersey GM. I can tell you that I never sat down to talk shop with anyone like Max McNab, and I never left our meeting without having learned something about hockey from this very knowledgeable and generous man.

One important lesson that I learned from him was that you can never have too many goalies or defensemen. You are going to suffer injuries, and if you don't have backup in those positions, you are going to be in trouble.

I also liked the way he helped the players, and their families. I liked the way he treated them. He was a real gentleman. As a GM, he had to make tough decisions. He had to release players, or not give them a raise, and navigate all that unpleasant stuff. But everything he did was with class, and I learned from that as well.

We had a season with ups and downs, but Kirk Muller scored twenty-two goals, and we beat Gretzky and the Cup champion Oilers at home, which was a big win for us. It looked like we were going in the right direction, as we finished in second-to-last place in the Patrick Division with 54 points, one point ahead of last-place Pittsburgh. The following year, we finished last, with 59 points, and missed the playoffs again. If we had been playing in the Smythe Division out west, we would have been in the postseason festivities, as the Vancouver Canucks finished with the same point total as we did, but their division was weaker and so they made it into the playoffs.

My Brooklyn past came to visit me one night in the parking lot at the Meadowlands, where the Devils played their home games at the Brendan Byrne Arena. A black limo with tinted windows pulled up next to me, and the window went down. Inside the limo was Chalky-Chalk, the Mafia guy who earned his nickname by only wearing white clothes, and who had gone to Detroit with the chop shop guy my brother's wife's uncle knew to kill Jimmy Hoffa.

I don't know who else was in the limo with them, and I didn't want to know. Chalky-Chalk said, "Hey Louie, you're playing Detroit tonight, who's injured on your team?" I just kept walking. I knew that the NHL had ex-FBI guys that were security for the teams, and they could be listening in on this. I was so pissed off that they thought I would give them inside information so they could use it however they planned. I didn't say a word to him. I just kept walking, and he kept pleading, "Come on, Louie, you can tell me."

I was angry. I called my brother Jerry who called his mother-in-law who called her brothers, and she told them straight out. She said, "If I freaking hear you bothered Louie ever again, I will come down there with my baseball bat and smash it over your stupid heads. Leave him alone. He's not involved in any of this." And they left me alone and never bothered me again.

Something which bothered me a lot is what made me leave the Devils in the end. I don't want to be coy and not tell you what it was about, but I am not going to elaborate because to do so will damage the reputation of a couple people and I don't want to do that to them. Let's just say that I had a different hockey philosophy than what I was seeing, and it compelled me to depart, and leave it at that.

When I told Dr. McMullen that I was moving on, he was so disappointed. He said, "No, I'm not accepting this. Could you come to the rink? I have pizza and a big screen TV. And the Astros are opening up this season." He wanted to talk to me.

Now I lived 50 miles away from the arena because I couldn't afford a house close to it. So I drove there, and it was just me and Dr. McMullen in the TV room along with the equipment guy, who went off to pick up the pizzas for us. We were sitting there, and McMullen said, "Look me in the eye, Lou. You're my Tommy Lasorda. I don't want you to leave. You do good for this organization. You're good for me. Max loves you. Thinks the world of you. Don't leave."

I couldn't tell him the reason why I couldn't or wouldn't work under the conditions I was experiencing at the Devils anymore, and I didn't want to put Max in any peril, so I drafted Joni into the story, which wasn't a big lie. I told McMullen that if I stayed, I would be divorced. I told him that my wife didn't want to live in New Jersey, which was true. She had no family there.

We were living miles out by the Delaware Water gap, and she was home with our infant son while I was on the road for two weeks at a time even when we were playing at home. I was always scouting other teams that we were going to play next because Doug Carpenter would say, "The

Rangers are at home tonight against Vancouver. I want you to go watch the game."

I would leave my house at seven in the morning with a newborn sleeping in his crib and go to the Devils practice. After practice, I would go to the office at Brendan Byrne Arena. I would do my paperwork there, as I had a lot of responsibilities. I handled all the travel for the team, and I would also go through all the game and player statistics.

And then I would drive into Manhattan and find a place to park near Madison Square Garden. Craig Patrick was the Rangers' GM and would always set me up in the press box. I would watch the Rangers play Vancouver and then drive home and arrive at one in the morning. Next day I would do it all again.

It was no fun for Joni, who was a new mother who really knew nobody in what was a hostile environment. In Colorado Springs everybody was polite, which in those days, was a much smaller place than it is today. People knew each other. They would wish you a good day and mean it, or offer help if you were shopping at Sears, and mean that, too.

I remember the first time we went to Sears in New Jersey. Joni wanted to get a washer and dryer for our New Jersey residence. There was a clerk sitting behind the desk in that department and Joni walked in front of the desk and cleared her throat and the clerk looked up and snarled "What!?"

It terrorized Joni, and she was in tears. She told me that she didn't think she could deal with the people in New Jersey, who she found so rough. And she had put up with two years of it, and now McMullen knew I was serious about leaving.

He said, "How are you going to get back home to Colorado Springs?"

I said, "I don't know. I don't have a car. I used the car you guys gave me when you hired me." It was a Ford Bronco.

I told him that my way home was not going to be a straight line. I wanted to go to Florida to see my family, as at that time, I had a lot of family down there. And then we would swing through New Orleans for some jazz and Cajun cuisine, and then go on up to Texas to see Joni's family.

He said, "Look, why don't you do this. I have a house, vehicles, maid service, and everything in Vail, Colorado. You're welcome to stay there until you figure out what you are going to do."

I thanked him but said no, that we would stay with Joni's parents, who had a big house and would put us up for a few months until we had sorted out our next move.

Dr. McMullen nodded, and then said, "Okay, take the Bronco with you and charge the gas to us. We will take care of it. Before you go, have the car completely checked out and stay at hotels anywhere along the way. We'll give you whatever the meal money is per day for this trip, and we'll double it." He smiled. "You and your wife and the baby don't eat much."

I mean, how could you not love people like that? I accepted, but I asked him how he planned to get the car back. He said that he would send Chris, one of the team's massage guys out to pick up the Bronco and drive it back. He would give him $1,000 to do it. Chris was thrilled beyond belief. He would have driven that car around the world.

But now, I was back in Colorado Springs, thinking about what I would do next. Was I done with hockey? Was it time to start that restaurant? Or would something else pop up that I hadn't expected? You guessed it. Something else popped up. And soon, I would be coaching hockey on the other side of the world.

CHAPTER 10

Going Back to My Roots

I WAS BACK IN COLORADO SPRINGS ONCE AGAIN TRYING TO FIGURE OUT my next move. Joni was pregnant with our second child, and just like the first time when she was pregnant with our son Brian, I would get an offer to uproot my family once again in the name of hockey. And like the previous time, it was an offer that I couldn't refuse.

Bob Johnson had been fired from coaching the Calgary Flames and was now the executive director of USA Hockey, which he had so christened. He called me up to tell me that they were hosting the International Ice Hockey Federation meeting at the Broadmoor hotel, and they wanted to invite me and Joni to attend the dinner.

So we went. It was a magnificent, elegant evening, and there were all kinds of people from the world's ice hockey federations there, and I knew them all. We sat at a table with the splendid Soviet goalie Vladislav Tretiak on whom I had once scored a goal, and Dummy Smit from Holland and his wife, Ilsa.

Smit had an international career as a player and a coach, and he had helped organize the Dutch team to play in Lake Placid for the Olympic Games, and then in the World Championships a year later. He was the technical director of the Dutch ice hockey association, but he had been a fine player, lacing up his skates for the Amsterdam Ice Birds after World War II. He'd played and coached internationally, and he was a good guy.

While we were at dinner, Dummy said to me, "Lou. Do you want to coach in Holland next year?" He knew that I had left the Devils. "I don't know," I said. "I think we're going to open a restaurant."

Dummy was amused by that. He said, "Come on! You're a hockey man. And if you coach the Tilburg Trappers and the Dutch national team, we can pay well. We're not like other European countries. We're Dutch and we're good with money. We would pay you in guilders, but it would be equal to US dollars, right?"

He told me the salary was $30,000 and that was the same as I had been making with the Devils, except in this case, the Dutch would pay taxes on my salary, not me. It would be tax-free. He told me that Tilburg was a lively town, about an hour and a half south of Amsterdam. Then he emphasized something that was music to my ears. "Our country is small, about the same size as Rhode Island. You can drive from one end to the other in three hours. You will sleep in your own bed every night."

He went on to tell me that since I would also be coaching the Dutch national team, I would be taking the team to the World Championships, which were going to be in northern Italy. It all sounded like a perfect solution to the question of what I would do next.

Joni wasn't so sure. She was due to deliver our second child on December 1. Our firstborn, Brian, was just two years old. Moving to a new country was exciting, and also daunting. She spoke to Ilsa, Dummy's wife, and Ilsa was lovely. Like all Dutch people, they spoke English perfectly. Ilsa told Joni she would take care of her, and take her shopping in Amsterdam, and it would all be a wonderful adventure. Joni really liked Ilsa and felt comfortable with her, and so a day later, I agreed to go to the Netherlands and continue my coaching career.

We went to Tilburg, and I loved it. It's a charming city in the southern province of North Brabant, and had about 175,000 people when we were there, so it was a bit smaller than Colorado Springs. But it was in Europe, and I could drive across the country in three hours. The Dutch people were welcoming and hospitable, and the team was rich in tradition and had a fair amount of talent. They had been founded in 1938, and had a long pedigree, with a few championships to their name. The kids I coached at hockey were keen to learn and to develop their skills. It was the perfect union of what I taught and what they wanted to learn, as I didn't have to "undo" anything that was already in their hockey baggage.

My son Greg was born in Tilburg. And his birth showed us a much better health program than we had in the United States. For one week before Joni went into labor, a doctor and a nurse came to our house to examine her and to make sure all was well. Greg was born on December 1, and I went to City Hall the next day and registered his birth and so he had Dutch citizenship, as well as American.

Joni only stayed in the hospital for one night. And they didn't take the baby away from her. They left Greg in bed with his mother. That's what you should do. And she loved it. Then, for two weeks after we got home, the nurse came to our house every day to check on Joni and Greg as part of their postnatal care. We saw how efficient this state-run medical system was, and it was very impressive and very much appreciated.

Like Dummy had said, I would come home after every game, and I got to spend much more time with my family than I had done in New Jersey. The only time I was gone was at the end of the year with the national team. We flew Joni's mother to Holland, and she spent a few days with us in Tilburg, and then I headed off with the team to the World Championships, and Joni and Greg, then about five months old, and Brian, then almost three, went back to the United States while I was in Italy. And so I ended up coaching in Italy at the World Championships. I felt right at home.

Our team was good, and we were doing well at the World Championships in Canazei, an alpine resort town in the Val di Fassa. I had been to Italy several times, but not here, which is in the far north of the country, near the Austrian border. When we pulled into the town I saw the sign, "Canazei," but beneath it was another word, "Cianacei." I asked what that was, and I learned it was the name of the town in Ladino, a language spoken by 8,000 people in the world, who lived in this valley. I can speak Italian, and was aware of the regional variations, which I knew from my own Southern Italian family. But in Canazei, when I would hear the local people speak, I couldn't understand a word because they were speaking Ladino. And they still do to this day.

When I was at the tournament, I was approached by two guys from Switzerland. They said, "We want to offer you a job coaching in Switzerland. And we'll pay you in US dollars, $80,000." Then the Swiss guy pulled out a big bank roll of $100 bills. He said, "I'll give you a signing bonus of $8,000 right now if you agree."

I told him I had to talk to my wife who was at home in Colorado, and there was a nine-hour time difference, so I had to wait a while. They agreed, and I called her. She asked me how Italy was, and I told her I was at a beautiful ski resort. Joni loved skiing. I told her that I didn't know what to do. "This team from Switzerland is offering a lot of money, Joni." It was almost triple what I was making in the Netherlands.

She asked me if I was comfortable with the Swiss guys. I said, "No. I don't like them. They're arrogant. They think I can be bought." I didn't like it when they whipped out that $8,000 in cash, as if I would just leap at the money. It offended me.

I understood enough Italian and spoke enough Italian that I could have basic conversations with people. Signor Scola was the president of the hockey team there, and he was also hosting this tournament. So when he came up to me in the rink and started speaking to me in Italian, asking me what I was going to do next year, I told him that I didn't know.

He then told me that two players who had played for me back in the United States were now playing here in Italy. He said that they were going to try to find me to say hello. I said I'd love to see them. And he said to me, "They respect you very much, and they like you. They think you'd be a great fit here. I want you to become our coach for the Sporting Hockey Club Fassa."

I was surprised, and I told him that I had to speak to my wife. He was a shrewd operator, and he asked me if she liked to ski. I told him that she did. He told me that it only cost $60 US to ski for a day pass and he would make that part of my contract, for my wife and my children. Then he closed his pitch with blood. "We know you have Italian blood. You know how we Italians are. We're family people and good honest people. And we'll make sure your kids are happy and you're happy and your wife is happy."

I called Joni and I told her that I had been asked to coach in Italy, and that it wasn't for much more money than we were getting in Holland but that he wanted me there in the middle of August, and the season ended at the end of March. "Then we're free. We can go home. And you know, Joni, they'll give us health insurance, and a nice apartment and a car. And ski passes. So it's not a bad deal. And again, I'll be home every night. I won't have to go on road trips."

Joni said, "Sign it, Lou. I want to go." So a happy wife is a happy life. I had to be polite to the people from Switzerland. They asked me again. And I told them that I had discussed it with my wife, and that she had said if they doubled the contract, and doubled the signing bonus, we would do it. I knew they would not, and I was right.

I said, "Gentlemen, thank you for coming here. I am honored. I appreciate your interest, and I wish you and your club the best success. But I can't become your coach."

The next morning, I told Signor Scola that I was on board, and he was delighted. He hosted a little reception for me, and I met a lot of other people, and I met players that I had coached before, and it was a fine reunion. That's how I ended up in Italy.

They were devastated when I left Holland. I loved it in Tilburg. I had really good friends, and I loved the local kids. But I had to go to Italy, and the Dutch were very disappointed. They weren't mad at me. They treated me with the utmost respect. But I told them that I had to do it as it was for more money, and my wife loved to ski.

They understood, but said that by leaving, I had also left them without a coach. They told me that I had brought them the greatest hockey season they had seen in years, and everyone liked me. There was only one response to that. I told them that I would get them a better coach.

They were puzzled by that. How could I get them a better coach for the same amount of money? Who would I get?

I had one answer. "How about Fred Shero?"

Fred was with the New Jersey Devils' radio highlight man when I was the assistant coach for the Devils. I didn't hang out with Doug Carpenter, but I hung out with Fred. I knew him when he coached the Philadelphia Flyers to their Stanley Cups in the 1970s.

One night we played in Chicago, and Fred and I were having a beer after the game. We were in the hotel bar, and it was late at night. I asked him if he missed coaching hockey, and he told me that he did. "But I can't do the NHL anymore," he said. "It would be too much."

I asked him where he would like to coach. He said, "I'd love to gig in Europe. You know, and not a top hockey country. I would just love to be in Europe."

I remembered that conversation when I was leaving Holland and told the Dutch that I would call Fred Shero to see if he was interested. I did, and he said, "Oh, I'd love it. Me and Mariette would love it." And then I called the Dutch people and put them on the phone with Fred and in two minutes, the deal was done. The great Fred Shero followed me as the coach of the Tilburg Trappers.

And I went to Italy. Joni absolutely loved it. So did my kids. I was there for three years in Val di Fassa and another two in Milan; Brian, my eldest, started school in Italy. He was learning Ladino and Italian. And he was learning German, since because of the proximity to Germany and Austria, many people in Canazei speak some German, too.

It is one of the most beautiful places in the world to live. The Dolomite mountains surround you, and you inhale the freshest air, and it's spectacular. The people were kind and hospitable to us, and I loved my team.

I had a lot of local kids, and I played them. The team president Scola was mad at me. He said, "We're paying three foreigners a lot of money to play here. Why play the locals?" I told him that we didn't have to win every game, we had to win the right games. We wanted to make the play-offs and do well in them. "You guys have suffered in the standings," I said. "But I'm going to go with the local kids because this is Italian hockey, and they deserve to play in their own country."

I told him not to worry, that I would use the three foreigners, but that they were not going to play every minute of every game. "That's just not my style. And it takes a team to win, not three players."

He was mumbling and grumbling at me, but all of a sudden, we went from being a .500 club to winning four games in a row against good opposition, and some of those games on the road. And these local kids were making a difference. They were getting confidence. They were happy. They felt respected, and I am very close to them to this day. The highlight of their life was that a coach trusted them to play the game to their best in their own country. Isn't that a strange concept?

When I coached Fassa, our longest road trip was to Milan, which is about a seven-hour drive. Most trips were not that pleasant because we had to drive through the Dolomite mountains in little buses on snowy mountain roads teeming with wildlife. You felt like you were taking your life in your hands.

We had two wonderful bus drivers. Guido did the long trips in the large bus. And the shortest trips in a smaller bus were made by Ferruccio. One time, going up through the mountains to go over one of the passes in the smaller bus, we slipped on a curve just outside of Val di Fassa. The back of the bus was right at the edge of the road. It was precarious.

We were all petrified, and Ferruccio said, "Don't move, nobody move." Slowly he directed the people in the back of the bus to walk to the front of the bus so the weight would be placed on the front wheels. Then he had us exit carefully, one after another. We stood on the side of the road with our backs against the mountain.

Ferruccio was the only one left on the bus, and he got it straightened out and back on the road again. The Italians have a sense of humor, and when he told nobody to move, he paused, then added, "*Conserva i panini!*" Or "Save the sandwiches!" Everybody was laughing in the face of doom, because Ferruccio wanted us to have sandwiches on the trip home. If we were going to drop 4,000 feet to our death, we might as well go down laughing.

I coached mostly in my broken Italian. Sometimes I would make a mistake and the players would giggle. Nobody spoke English other than some imported players. Nobody spoke English in the whole town. I was certain that the kids that I had as players couldn't speak a word of it. When I went back to Canazei four or five years ago for a visit, they all conversed in English. And that's because of the internet. Across Europe, everyone speaks English.

Of course, Joni tried her best to learn Italian. One day I came home, and she was in tears. She said, "I'm never shopping again." I asked her what had happened.

She was planning to make minestrone soup. She learned the recipe from one of the women over there. And it was delicious, but she had to shop for ingredients, and in those days, there were no big supermarkets in the Val di Fassa. If you wanted vegetables or fruit, you would go to the vegetable or fruit shop. If you wanted cheese, you went to the cheese shop. If you wanted meat, you went to the butcher shop.

Joni enjoyed this shopping scenario because it also created a social life. You got out to see other people, your neighbors and friends. You might even stop and have an espresso, or a cappuccino. So Joni told me that to make the soup, she needed half a head of small cabbage. There was a line of people behind her in the shop, and when it was her turn, she was nervous. She told them what she needed, in Italian, and everybody burst out laughing.

I asked her what she had said. She said that she needed "*mezza testa di cavolo*," which means half a head of cabbage. But it didn't come out that way. It sounded like she said "*cavallo*" instead of "*cavolo*" and "*cavallo*" means horse in Italian. To the people in the shop, it sounded as if she had said she needed half a horse's head. That's why they were laughing.

I told her that every day I made a million mistakes. I said things that made no sense whatsoever. It was part of the learning process. I told her that my players loved making fun of me behind my back, and it was all in good fun. And if it was reversed, you would be laughing, too. You endeared yourself to them.

The next time Joni had to go to the vegetable shop, she asked me to come with her. I did and the saleswoman had the biggest grin on her face when she saw us. They were going outside their zone a bit and selling a special salami from Calabria, and she went and sliced five slices of it and some fresh bread and put the salami on the bread for Joni and me. She was speaking as she worked and said, "I hope I didn't offend you the other day. But what you said just struck me as funny and so, please forgive me." She couldn't have been sweeter. And she and Joni became friends. They would meet for coffee and Joni would work on her Italian, so it had a happy ending.

I went to Milan to coach HC Milano Saima after my third year at Canazei. Milano had been promoted from the B league to the A league in 1988 and had asked me if I'd come and run their team in Serie A. They offered me double the salary that I was making at Fassa, so I had to do it for my family's well-being. It wasn't a fortune, but it was pretty good money for seven months of work. It was a challenge, but I knew we could win the championship.

In Milan, I inherited a masseur, a Russian guy named Alex. He would work for the Montreal Canadiens in the NHL. Alex came to me and said, "Coach. I have a friend named Yuri Karmanov. He's a former player in the Soviet top league, and he played in the European champions, and was roommates with Vladislav Tretiak. Vladislav played most of the games in goal, and Yuri was his backup. But he played for Tarasov, then he went on to play for other teams. And he's living in Milan now. And he asked me if I would talk to you about the possibility of interviewing him for an assistant coach's position if you have one."

I went to the general manager and asked, "Can we hire him? Can we pay him?" He said sure, we can pay him, so Yuri met with me and immediately I liked him. He was a real gentleman. He was very educated. His father was a colonel in the Red Army. His mom was the head of a music institute in Moscow.

He was very well-dressed, and very articulate in English. He spoke Russian, of course, and he spoke English, a little bit of Italian, and he was learning Czech. So this was a smart man. And we became great friends. I helped him get a job in the NHL scouting with the St. Louis Blues after our team folded in Italy. We were more than friends. We were brothers.

Another guy who was like family was Gerry Ciarcia. I brought him from Fassa with me. He was one of the players that I had them sign, and as part of the deal to move to Milan I told them that I wanted to have Gerry, who was a good, steady defenseman.

He was from Boston and became a naturalized Italian. He played in the NCAA with Bowdoin College, and between 1979 and 1981 he played in the Central Hockey League with the Oklahoma City Stars, and in the Eastern Hockey League with the Baltimore Clippers. After that he moved to Italy to play in the Italian League, where he spent the rest of his career.

When he played for me at the Sporting Hockey Club Fassa, I got close to him, and our families were tight. Joni and his wife were friends.

We made the playoffs, and in the final playoff game against Bolzano Foxes for the championship of Italy, with five or six minutes to go, I benched Gerry because he was having trouble pivoting. They had some really good players, especially Gates Orlando and Perry Turnbull, who had both played in the NHL. They had beaten Gerry to the outside a couple of times in the game.

This was a chance to win a championship, and the last game of the playoffs with five minutes to go. I had another player who hadn't played very well in that game, but I thought I could motivate him. I said, "I need you to get out there and score the winner." He was a veteran centerman from Thunder Bay. And he went out there and he scored what turned out to be the winning goal. He scored right away, and 3–2 for us was enough to win the title.

So we won the game, and we won the championship and there were 12,000 spectators singing, and fireworks blasting, and you would think we had won the Stanley Cup and not the Italian Championship. But it was their first championship in forty years, and people were happy.

I shook hands with our players who were all celebrating. And I said, "Gerry, congratulations!" He wouldn't shake hands with me. He said, "You just ruined my life."

It was the worst feeling I could imagine. And he never said another word to me until December 2023. Thirty-one years later. And it really hurt me deeply. I really liked him and his family. One of the things you have to be as a coach is the guy who makes decisions that can help the team but not help a player. That is what I had done. So it hurt me, and I never forgot it. I often would think about it as unfinished business. I didn't know if he was dead or alive, or what happened to his family. Nothing. It just bothered me, but then, at the end of 2023, he sent me a text.

He lives in Massachusetts now. And this is what he said.

Merry Christmas and Happy New Year my old friend. It's been far too long. I asked Chip [that's Ron Chipperfield, the first captain of the Edmonton Oilers] *for your cell number. I hated the way Italy ended up but I certainly have thought my actions through.* Mark Johnson [former NHLer and coach at the University of Wisconsin] *had told me you never question a coach's decision. Mark was right. That being said, I respect and remember all the wonderful times we spent with you and your family in Fassa, and I also appreciate the extremely great coaching that I received from you. Best to you and your family would have a healthy 2024. Gerry.*

I wrote back:

Let's talk soon. I'm not good at texting, I'm happy to hear from you. And never forgot the good times. But the way it ended is very sad to me. You were more than just a player to me, a good player and a very nice person. I made a hockey decision. And at the same time I lost the person I greatly appreciated and respected. It was very difficult. I thought about you and your family all these years, and I'm very grateful to you for reaching out. I'll be 79 in February and still coach little guys, only off ice, no more skating. Very rewarding. Let's talk when you're ready.

I called him three or four hours after we texted. We spoke for an hour and a half. I talked to his wife, who was so delighted that we reconnected, and we shared some old-time stories. It was really very nice. And now an old wound had been healed with Gerry.

After we won that championship, I agreed to spend another year with Milano Saima. An intermediary for Silvio Berlusconi (who owned the Milano Devils) had been the general secretary of the Italian Ice Hockey Federation and was now working for the Milano Devils; he approached me with an offer. He told me that Berlusconi, rich from his media empire but not yet a politician, but soon would be in 1994, wanted me to sign with the Devils as their coach.

They were a good team and had some notable players. Jari Kurri of the Edmonton Oilers was playing for them in 1991, as he was trying to force a trade from Edmonton. Mark Napier, who had won two Stanley

Cups with the Oilers, was also on that team. But our team in Milan always beat the other team in Milan.

Berlusconi had seen me in action one very memorable day early in that championship season of ours. Our president, Massimo Moratti, came into our dressing room before our game against the Devils and asked very politely if he could talk to the team before the game. He was the president of the team, and I told him that of course he could speak to the guys.

He came into the middle of our dressing room. He went down on one knee, and he put his hands out in front of him as if he was praying. He was dramatic. Very Italian. He said, "I don't care if we don't win another game the whole year. But we have to win this game."

He and Berlusconi were archrivals, in business and in sport. Berlusconi owned AC Milan and Moratti owned the Inter Milan team, the two soccer teams who made international news when they played. And Moratti owned our team and Berlusconi owned our opponent. Both these owners wanted to win everything at any cost. It was personal between them. They couldn't be on the field or the ice, but they competed in the stands with each other.

So Moratti was down on one knee, telling the guys that he didn't care if they lost every game this season, to please just win this one. He had an assistant from Naples with him, and he motioned to the assistant to get on with the motivation part of the speech. The assistant then hauled out this brown paper bag, stuffed with cash.

He pulled out stacks of US$100 bills, with rubber bands around them. Moratti said, "If we win today by four goals or more, everybody gets $500. Everybody."

I wanted to make sure that he really meant everybody, so I interrupted him to ask if our trainer, Alex, a Russian who lived on US$500 a month and Yuri, my assistant coach, and our equipment guy, would also get $500. Moratti looked startled for just a second and told me he hadn't planned to give anything to them, but he looked at me and he said, "*Si! Si! Si!*" So I said, "Okay, come on, boys. Let's go out and make sure they lose by four or more."

The Devils had a former NHL goalie of Italian heritage, Roberto Romano. He was a good goalie, and he was starting in goal for them. I don't know if it was the money that did it or the loyalty to Marotti, but we came out like we were playing a bunch of little kids.

We chased their goalie Romano in the first period, and we were up six nothing after 20 minutes. We won that game 10–0, and Moratti was ecstatic. I took my $500, and I decided to go gambling with the assistant GM, Aldo, whose real name was Luciano, but I called him Aldo because he looked like a kid from my neighborhood whose name was Aldo. He was a taxi driver for a living.

This was early season, and Joni was back home in the United States with the kids because her mother had brain cancer so Joni was helping her. I said to Aldo that we should go to Campione, a casino, right across the lake from Lugano, Switzerland. It was an hour's drive.

So we went. You have to wear a jacket and a tie, and you have to pay 50,000 lire to get in, which was about $50. All the money I had to gamble with was the money I had unexpectedly received that day. I was, so to speak, playing on house money.

When we were leaving, the secretary at the rink asked us where we were going. We told her that we were going to Campione. She asked if we were going to play roulette, and we said we were. She told us to bet numbers three and twenty-one. Now I would never bet those numbers. Maybe I would bet twenty-one. But I hate number three. I don't know why. I just do.

At the casino, I went to the American table where the odds are a little against you because they have double zero and zero. But you can bet in US dollars. So, remembering what the secretary had said, I put $100 on number three, and $100 on number twenty-one. The croupier spun the wheel, and it landed right on three and I won $3,500. Right off the bat. I was stunned, in a very happy way.

Then I doubled my bet. I put $200 on number three, and I kept $100 on twenty-one. And they spun the wheel, and I couldn't even see what was happening because people were pushing and leaning in, and it was wild. I heard the croupier say *"Numero tre."* Number three had hit again.

I made $7,000 on that bet, and now had $10,000 in "free money." Aldo was telling me that it was time to go back to Milan with the winnings, but I said no. I was in a frenzy. So then I put $500 on twenty-one, and I left $200 on three. It hit twenty-one and I won $17,500.

Aldo really wanted me to leave now so I told him to be calm. I told him that I could not leave with a hot hand and as punctuation to that point, I gave him $1,000. That shut him up. We stayed about five or six hours, and then we left. When I got home and counted the cash, I had won $51,000.

We had another day off so I told Aldo that we should go to Venice and try our luck there. We took the train from Milan, and it was beautiful, early winter, but sunny and warmish. We walked along the Grand Canal, and we had a delicious lunch and then we went to the big casino on the Grand Canal.

Lou Nanne, the Minnesota North Star great, had told me that he played there once, and he won a ton of money betting on number twenty-three. That was the number on his jersey when he played. So I told Aldo I was going to bet $500 on twenty-three. It hit and I won $17,500. I gave Aldo two grand and kept playing and we walked out of there with $15,000. I had won $66,000 by gambling that $500 bonus money we had won for beating Berlusconi's team.

I called Joni the next day, first checking in with her about her mother, who was very ill with brain cancer. She was under stress, and I wanted to deliver some good news. I told her what happened at the casinos, and that stressed her out even more. She pleaded with me not to gamble anymore, and I promised her that I was done. I told her that I would start wiring my winnings home in increments of $9,000. I told her to buy that car that she wanted, a new Toyota Four Runner and to do the kids' rooms and get new carpeting. I told her to get whatever she wanted. And then I went back to coaching Saima, but now Silvio Berlusconi wanted me.

So the intermediary set up a meeting even though I told him I had already agreed to coach Milano Saima. He said, "It doesn't matter. Mr. Berlusconi wants to meet with you."

I went to this very nice trattoria by a canal to meet Berlusconi for lunch. It was very pleasant and nice, and I met Berlusconi and shook his hand and sat down. He got straight to the point. "You know, we would like you to coach our team this coming season."

I thanked him and told him that I was flattered by his proposal, but that I already agreed verbally with the owner of Milano Saimi to coach them. Berlusconi smiled at me, and I will never forget what he said, in Italian, because he did not speak English. He asked me if I had signed a contract. I told him no, not yet.

He grinned broadly and put his palms up and cocked his head and said, "*Allora, sei libero!*" Which means "Well, then, you're free." That's what he said. Then he added that he would pay me $20,000 more in cash than what Saima had offered. And if we won the championship, I would get another very big bonus. It was all very tempting.

I was making a fairly good salary by that point. It was not a lot of money, but it was certainly fair. They gave me a car, which was stolen four times because Milan had a problem with car thieves, so I finally gave up and started walking. Anyway, Berlusconi told me several times that I was free, and that I could sign with him and win for him. I kept saying no.

Finally, he could see that I wasn't going to break my word. I just couldn't. The last thing he said to me, as we sat face to face, was this: "Luigi. You are making a big mistake. But I appreciate your position. And I admire you for living up to what you feel is your word. It's not a good business decision and you wouldn't be breaking any rules. But I see what kind of heart you have. Even so, it's not a good business decision. I hope you don't regret it."

I regretted it for a few reasons. I could have probably made $40,000 to $50,000 more if I had gone to the Devils, because after that meeting they went out and bought some more fine players. But that's the way it goes. Anyway, I liked Berlusconi and told him that. I said, "You're a good guy and one day I could see you as president of Italy." And he rolled his eyes at that as if I was crazy to think it, and then he became president of Italy.

I also regretted not saying yes to him because the bums I gave and kept my word to at Saima folded on the last day of the season and stiffed me out of $5,000. And we lost the seventh game of the playoffs, in overtime, to Berlusconi's team.

We were cheated out of it. The head referee in the league was from Bolzano, and Bolzano hated the team I was coaching. And they really ran the league.

We were tied after regulation and after overtime, so we went to a shootout. Kevin Lavallee was our player, and he lost the puck momentarily on his penalty shot to tie the game. And can you imagine what happened next? A whistle came screeching from the stands, and it was the head referee blowing a whistle and yelling at the referee on the ice, telling him that the game was over because our player—just for a moment—lost control of the puck as he was going forward. Therefore, the penalty shot was disqualified.

The Milano Devils won. We protested, but nothing happened. And then our team folded after that game. And that was it. Everybody went home and I came home, too. Once again, not knowing what I was going to do with the rest of my life. I was about to turn fifty, and as I had done many times before, I had no idea what was coming next.

CHAPTER 11

A Special Project

ONCE AGAIN, I WAS BACK AT SQUARE ONE. RATHER, I WAS MAYBE AT square five or six, but I still had no plan for what I was going to do next in the summer of 1992. And then, once again my phone rang, and on the other end of it was Baaron Pittenger.

Pittenger had been the executive director of the US Olympic Committee, which he had joined in 1977 after serving as the Sports Information director at Brown University, and then at Harvard University, before moving up to be the associate director of athletics there. He was the guy who thought up the National Sports Festival in 1978. He was a very talented man, and a wise, educated, good human being. In 1990, he became executive director of USA Hockey, and that's why he was calling me now.

He heard that I had arrived back in Colorado Springs. He asked me where I was living, and it was close to his office, on 30th Street, close to the Garden of the Gods, a vast natural park with these amazing red rock formations and one of the highlights of the city. He invited me to lunch. I asked him when, and he said, "How about today?"

His office was a mile and a half from my house, and he suggested we meet there, and then go eat. I arrived at USA Hockey and said hello to a few of the people I had worked with before I departed for the New Jersey Devils, and then Baaron and I went to a lovely French restaurant called Marigold. And we had a delightful lunch.

During our meal, Baaron asked me how I felt about coming back to work for USA Hockey. He was supposed to be a temporary director, as he was pushing seventy, but he was now in his third year there, so I figured things might be a little shaky. When I had left USA Hockey, I was very clear that I did not want my old job back, so I asked him what he imagined that I would be doing. He said, "special projects."

Then he elaborated. He said, "Look, we're having internal problems. And Walter Bush, our president, wanted me to call you and offer you a job. He told me that 'Lou is tough enough to handle these internal problems.' You have credibility and you'll confront people who need to be confronted. We don't have anybody who will do that."

Now, when I'm wrong, I'll take full responsibility for being wrong and shut up. But when I'm right, I am not going to press my case. I knew I could take on whatever problems they had and solve them without too much destruction. So I said I would come back and see what I could do, even though Baaron did not offer much detail beyond "internal problems." I figured that someone was causing problems, and it would be a test to see if I could solve them.

I went back to USA Hockey, and it was the worst couple of years of my life, trying to find out where the problems were exactly. It took its toll. The salary wasn't very good, as it was much less than what I was making coaching hockey. But I was a mile and a half away from home, and you don't often have a job where you can jump in the car and go have lunch at home with your family and come back to the office, all within an hour.

I was comfortable with most of the people I was working with. But I eventually learned that there were some whom I had to confront, as they were part of the problem.

The problem was that people get used sometimes, and it affects the people around them. I don't want to name names here, but the major problem was a guy at USA Hockey who was being manipulated and used by people outside of the organization to the detriment of those within it. He was in a tough position, and I confronted the guy and recommended that USA Hockey fire him immediately. And they did.

Once USA Hockey got this "inside" person out, then it was much easier to deal with the people who were manipulating him on the outside. I felt bad because I had hired this person and thought a lot of him. He had been an excellent administrator, and he did a great job. But he got a little power hungry and that allowed him to be manipulated by some bad actors, who all ended up failing in the end. I am happy to say that this guy and I are very close again today, and I'm helping him with different things. He's a talented person. He admitted to me that he was manipulated and used, and it pissed him off. But I am very happy we are friends again.

It was a tough period of my life at home as well. We noticed our kids weren't doing too well. They were suffering from depression. My marriage was failing as well, and before long, I would be divorced. It was a stressful time, and I knew I was not doing anything wrong. At least professionally, I was doing what I believed was the right thing to do for the good of hockey in my country.

My goal also was to protect the president, Walter Bush, and Baaron Pittenger and USA Hockey and the good things they were doing, and the good things that I think I did there for nearly the next thirty years.

One of the best things I did when I returned to USA Hockey was reconnecting with Willie O'Ree, the first Black player to lace up his skates in the NHL, which he did for the Boston Bruins on January 18, 1958. I had seen Willie play at Madison Square Garden when he caught on with the Bruins in the 1960–1961 season, but the story goes back further than that.

When I was a kid living in the projects in Brooklyn, my best friend happened to be a Black kid named Ralph Dease. He was a good athlete, but he wouldn't play roller hockey with us. And I would ask him all the time to play roller hockey with us. And Ralph said, "Negroes don't play hockey." That's what Black people called each other in those days, and white people did as well, if they were polite.

And we were polite in my family, as my mother would have killed us if we had used any kind of racial or ethnic slur. "We don't look down on anybody, and we certainly don't use those kinds of words," is what she said, and so, we did not.

I took Ralph to see the Rangers playing the Bruins in 1960, when we were fifteen years old, and he saw Willie O'Ree, and so he saw that Black people did, in fact, play hockey, and play it very well. So Ralph started playing hockey with us after that because he had seen a Black guy play it, and one who became his role model.

Bryant McBride was a Black guy born in Chicago and adopted by a Canadian family in Sault Sainte Marie, Ontario. He grew up in Canada. He played hockey, and went to prep school in Maine, then to West Point, where he played on the varsity soccer and hockey teams for the Cadets. He transferred to Trinity College in Connecticut, and played sports there, too.

He became the vice president of business development for the National Hockey League in 1991, and the first African American hired by the NHL in an executive role. In 1993 he created the NHL/USA Hockey Diversity Task Force (now known as Hockey Is for Everyone).

The way USA Hockey connected with the NHL was due to Bryant giving me a call. He had learned that USA Hockey had started an inner-city hockey program and they wanted to help. I was thrilled to have them join us. Between Bryant and NHL Commissioner Gary Bettman, they pumped a lot of money into that inner-city program. They put more money into the program than did USA Hockey, and they had more money than us. They put their money where their mouth was, and I will always respect Bryant and Bettman for doing that, for giving players who otherwise would not have had the chance an opportunity to experience this beautiful game.

At the time that we started it, in the early 1990s, there might have been three or four players of color in the NHL. Today we are getting close to forty, so I would humbly say that our program had success. USA Hockey originated the idea, but the NHL powered it. We couldn't do what they did. So it worked out. It was a perfect marriage.[1]

We were in a meeting one day, talking about how Jackie Robinson had broken the color barrier when he joined the Brooklyn Dodgers in 1947. I mentioned that the NHL had their own Jackie Robinson, and his name was Willie O'Ree. In fact, I would later learn that Willie had met Jackie Robinson twice, once when Willie was a kid and his baseball team had won the championship of their hometown, Fredericton, New Brunswick. Their prize was a trip to New York City, where they went to a Brooklyn Dodgers game, and afterward, the players met Jackie.

Willie told Jackie that he also played hockey and was going to play in the NHL. Jackie was surprised and said that there were no Black players in that league. Wilie told him he would be the first. So he was, and when Willie was playing pro hockey, he met Jackie Robinson again at an NAACP event, and Jackie remembered.

Everyone in the room was amazed to learn that hockey had its own Black pioneer. It has had many, in fact, but Willie was the first to play in the NHL. No one else, including Bryant, knew who Willie was, partly because they were probably too young, and partly because the NHL had not yet done the wonderful job that it would do to make Willie and his achievement known to the world.

They wondered if he was still alive. I said I would find out. I was very good friends with a guy who coached Willie when he played in the Western League, Max McNab, one of the greatest hockey men I've ever known or met. Max assured me that Willie was alive and well, and he was living in San Diego.

I told Bryant the good news, and he contacted John Halligan, who once worked for the Rangers and was now working for the NHL with alumni. They knew some FBI guys in San Diego, and asked them to find Willie. I can only imagine his surprise when he was contacted by the FBI, as he's such a law-abiding guy. In fact, he had been working as a security guard in San Diego when we caught up with him.[2] Next thing you know, the NHL hired him.

I first met Willie in Boston, as we were doing a diversity clinic up there, and the NHL brought Willie in. I didn't go up to Willie and say, "Hey Willie! I recommended you for this job!" I only talked about seeing him play, and how he inspired my friend Ralph to take up hockey. He was very professional and gracious. He came from a wonderful family. And he's a good human being.

I don't know how he found out that I had recommended him. But I do know that he went from being a night watchman making not much money in San Diego to an executive position with the NHL and new-found and much-deserved fame. The NHL role greatly benefited him and his family, and as the NHL's diversity ambassador, he did a wonderful job, connecting with kids and their families across North America, delivering the message that yes, hockey is for everyone.

This Jackie Robinson of hockey treated everyone with dignity and respect, and he was truly colorblind. He saw everyone as a person and treated them all in that golden rule kind of way. I was thrilled to get close to him, and to his wife, Deljit. I love them. I'm so happy that he's been recognized as a member of the Hockey Hall of Fame, that his jersey was retired by the Bruins, that the US Congress gave him the Congressional Gold Medal, and that the Canadian government issued both a silver coin and a postage stamp in his honor.

Two summers ago, we did a showcase in Colorado Springs for young players. It was on a Thursday night, and I was sitting in the hallway of the arena when I saw this big, tall Black kid walk in. I asked him if he was here for the hockey showcase, and he said he was.

I asked him where he was from, and he told me he was from Chicago. I knew he had to be a good player, or he wouldn't have been invited. I said, "I'm really happy to see you here. We don't get many Black kids from Chicago."

He said that he just had to get into hockey, and so I invited him to pull up a chair and tell me his story. I asked him how he got involved with the game.

He said, "I just love hockey; I saw it on television, and I just loved it."

I asked him if he had ever heard of Willie O'Ree, and his eyes lit up. "Yes! That's why I am here. I was watching TV and I saw a hockey game. I watched the game, and I liked it. Then they did an interview with Willie O'Ree, and I was amazed. I didn't know that Black people played hockey. So I told my parents, and they supported me on it. They, and Willie O'Ree, got me into hockey, and here I am."

I was delighted to hear this. The kid told me that his father had even bought a jersey signed by Willie O'Ree at an auction.

I said, "What a great story. Hold on a second." And I took out my phone and I called Willie, and he answered. He was happy to hear from me. I told him that I was sitting with a young Black man from Chicago who was in Colorado Springs for the showcase in hockey. "I know he wouldn't be invited if they didn't think he was really good. And he's blaming you for taking up hockey! You inspired him, and his father's got an autographed jersey of yours and so would you like to say hello to him?" Willie said that he would very much like to do that, so I handed the phone to the kid and said, "Willie wants to talk to you."

He looked as if his dream had just come true. He took the phone as if it was the holy grail and put it to his ear and said hello, shyly and with reverence. And then Willie worked his magic. He asked the kid what position he played. Center ice. Willie asked him if he liked to pass the puck. "I would rather score a goal," the kid replied. I really started laughing. And they had about a five- or six-minute conversation. This kid was so psyched up by this unexpected conversation with his hero.

I've done that with about a half a dozen kids of color I have met on the ice. I have called Willie and let these kids talk to him as well. And Willie always gives them his time and he inspires them, and then they do the same for other kids.

Last year, I coached a bantam team. I had two or three kids of color on my team. So I set up a Zoom call with Willie. And I invited their parents and all the kids on the team to join us on the big TV at the rink. They spoke to Willie live from his house in San Diego, and he had each kid stand up and introduce themself. He had a really fine conversation with all the kids, and they asked him a ton of questions, and he answered them all.

It was very important for both the kids of color and the white kids on the team. It's important that all the families are together because it's how you unite people. We're all in this sport together, so let's support each other.

My own sons played hockey and loved it. They were both good athletes. Brian was an outstanding hitter in baseball and had a very sweet swing of the bat. Greg was a clever little hockey player. He wasn't the best skater, but he handled the puck well and he was unselfish, always looking to make a play. Brian could skate and was big and strong and a very smart player, and they were both good teammates. They pleased me as a hockey coach.

Of course, I never actually coached them because you can't coach your own kids. It's almost impossible. One time I was teaching Greg how to play T-ball out front of the house in Colorado Springs. He was about five years old at the time, and I had told him that he had to hold his hands a certain way and had to keep his eye on the ball. Then when the time is right, you hit the ball and follow through.

I was setting up the ball on the tee and I was being very patient, but he was stubborn, and he was going to do it his way and just hack at it. Finally, I yelled at him. I said, "Dammit, Greg! Do what I tell you! Don't argue with me! I'm a professional coach!"

He leaned back, with one hand on the knob of his bat, and he looked at me and said, "Oh yeah, but that's in hockey. And I heard you weren't even very good at that."

I was livid. He took off running, and I chased after him. We lived in a cul-de-sac, and he ran through our neighbors' yards, and I couldn't catch him. He was weaving and running, and Joni came out and asked, "What is going on? You can't be chasing your kid around people's yards over something so stupid like that." She was right. I never said another word to the boys regarding sports.

In fact, when I went to their games, I went alone, and I never said a word to the coaches. I just watched as far away as I could and still be able to see the play. And at the end of the year, every year, in whatever sport they were playing, I would bring a bottle of wine in a brown paper bag with me, and I would walk up to the coach, whom I had never met or talked to. I would hand him the bag and say, "This is for you, Coach. Thank you for what you're doing for all the kids. It's appreciated." And I would walk away. I've been there. Parents love their kids, and their kids are never going to be wrong. I get it.

I have to admit that while I was in my first stretch back at USA Hockey, I was losing support at home, and Joni and I were heading for divorce. It was the residual effect of my life in hockey.

When we were in Italy, Joni's mother had brain cancer and had to go into a care home, and it eventually killed her. And Joni was afraid that her father would be struggling on his own. Our kids were getting older and her father, who didn't butt into our marriage, did make a comment one time that changed things. He said, "Well, I got two little Italian grandsons, or I got two little American grandsons. I don't know if they're going to remember how to speak English."

He hinted that maybe it was time for the kids to go to school in their home country. They were happy in Italy, and they didn't complain, but I knew that Joni needed to be back home for her father. So I said, "What do you want to do? Do you want to stay home?"

She said, "Yes. I think I'll get them settled in school."

So she and the boys stayed in the United States for two seasons while I was coaching in Milan. And it probably contributed to what happened next. A married couple cannot be separated like that for four or five months. It was tough.

Our marriage lasted only ten years, unfortunately. We realized that we had some issues with our kids' mental health, as they both suffered from depression, and that put a big strain on Joni, especially with my constant coaching travel and my own stressful situations that coaching can produce.

Our thirteen-year age difference started to show as well, in the sense that different generational values started to bubble up. We never had that problem before we got married, but now we did. She felt she needed some personal time for herself, or for us to go on a ski trip together. Her passion was skiing. I was still doing some coaching, and as a result, I wasn't allowed to ski because I could break a leg or an ankle and that would take me out of my game.

I didn't want to go anywhere. I loved being with my kids every chance I had, but of course, that's all she did was be with the kids every day. In any kind of a breakup, it's never one person's fault. Sometimes it's nobody's fault. My personal philosophy is simply that sometimes what you thought was love might have been infatuation, and while it started everything, it just wears out. There's not much left after that. Joni's interests were different from mine. The only thing we really truly had in common were our kids. She didn't really care about hockey. And I wasn't into skiing and dancing.

I don't regret it. She's a good person. And we're still very good friends. Our breakup, however, was very hurtful to me, and it was Joni who divorced me. I didn't divorce Joni, and I would not have, if for no other reason than I didn't want to lose my kids.

Even divorced, we went through a lot with the boys, and we did it together. We tried to be as good as we could be for the boys.

So at the turn of the twenty-first century, I was divorced, still with USA Hockey, and still devoted to the game. I was running the hockey development camps. I feel that this was how I really contributed to the improvement of hockey in the United States. These development camps, or identification camps with some development, opened an opportunity for kids from every state to be seen on the ice, and to learn by playing against kids from all the other states. It really accelerated the development of a national hockey culture for young players on their way up.

I went back to Minnesota to run a development camp in St. Cloud, and Herb Brooks was working as a scout for the Pittsburgh Penguins, and we bumped into each other at the rink in St. Cloud. We hadn't talked in more than a decade, and Herb was not the easiest guy to always get along with. I have the highest respect for him as a coach, and he's a very smart person. Nobody else could have won that gold medal in Lake Placid.

I was, however, distraught that Herb Brooks was at odds with USA Hockey. I didn't like reading that he was constantly knocking USA Hockey. He had some very valid points, many of which I agreed with, but he was using the magazine *Let's Play Hockey* as his vehicle to spew his criticisms. It was not the right way to do it. I felt he was taking cheap shots because USA Hockey wasn't able to defend itself.

So we greeted each other, and I said, "Herb, I need to tell you something." He had a minute, so I suggested that we go sit outside on a bench. "Nobody will bother us."

I said, "I'll make it fast. Listen, I had a very good visit with Tarasov a couple of years ago. And I said, 'Anatoly, do you have any regrets in life?' And he was an actor. He was dramatic. He couldn't just answer me. He had to put his glasses on the tip of his nose, rub his forehead, and do all those actions that an actor might do in order to convey gravitas. And he said, 'That's a very good question. That's profound.' But he hadn't answered me, so I asked him again."

"He said, 'Of course,' in Russian. I knew that word. 'But of course.' Then he told me what they were. He said, 'I made a big mistake. And it's a regret to this day that I fought with the Soviet Ice Hockey Federation. Make no mistake about it. They were wrong. But I didn't handle it well. I challenged them and I fought them. I didn't discuss it rationally with them. And it seemed like every week we were arguing over some point, and we wasted a lot of energy. It did me no good. It hurt me. And it did them no good. It hurt them. Nobody won. Shame on them and shame on me. If I was doing it over again, I would not have fought with the federation. It hurt hockey in my country.'"

I told Herb that it was profound for me to hear Tarasov say that. Herb highly respected Tarasov, and he respected me for writing to Tarasov and then going to meet him to learn from him. And then to bring him to the United States to do seminars. Herb was very grateful as an American because he knew that it had done a lot of good for our game, quite literally. Herb had played against Tarasov's teams when he was playing for the US national team. So he knew how good they were.

I could see that Herb was touched by my story. I told him that he was in a position to change things before it was too late, and to avoid making the mistake that Tarasov made. "You can come back and fix the problem," I said. "Instead of throwing darts at it from the outside. And I can be your conduit. Why don't you come to Colorado Springs in three weeks? We have our annual congress, and you can see for yourself how it operates."

I reminded him that the staff did not make the policies, so not to get mad at the staff. I reminded him that we were a not-for-profit, volunteer hockey program that had done some good for the country. I also said that this did not mean that we had not made mistakes. We had. "And that's where you come in," I said. "Consult with us. And you could help us. You can voice your opinions to the people who make the decisions. You might even get a gig out of it."

He listened, but he wasn't convinced. He told me that the Minnesota hockey group had told him they were against this policy and that one, "but you guys did it anyway."

I said, "Personally, if you would come to the meeting you'd help me, because I happen to agree with most of your criticisms. But you're directing them at the wrong people. If you come to the meeting, you'll see.

You'll sit in the audience next to me; we'll see how they vote and what they say and what they do."

He said he was late for an appointment, but that he would think about it, and then he left. He called me later on that day. He reached me in my St. Cloud College dorm room. He asked if we could meet for breakfast the next day. He would pick me up out front at 8 a.m.

While we ate breakfast, he told me that he thought my story about Tarasov was a fine one, and that he could see it made sense. And he said that he would come to Colorado Springs. I called my bosses and told them, and they were delighted. They said they would send tickets for him and his wife, Patti.

So he came west, and we honored him at a banquet, and he got to see the meetings in action. And it opened the door. A conversation began, and I mentioned that we had the Winter Olympics coming up in Salt Lake City. And then I made my pitch. "You know what would be wonderful, Herb? If you would coach the 2002 Olympic hockey team. Twenty-two years later you're back in the game."

He smiled, and he said, "I'd be interested." That's all I needed to hear. I told our people that we had to hire him. They agreed. Then Herb told me, "I want you on my staff, officially this time, as an assistant coach. Not like we did it in 1980. You'd be on the team."

I said I would be honored to do it, so long as I could do exactly what I did in 1980. I wanted to scout teams in advance, and watch games from upstairs with a walkie-talkie, or by 2002, on a headset connected to the bench, and meet with him between periods to tell him what I had seen. He agreed. I was going back to the Olympics one more time.

CHAPTER 12

The Olympic Last Hurrah

ONCE AGAIN, I WAS GETTING READY FOR AN OLYMPIC HOCKEY TOURNA-
ment, and once again, I was assisting Herb Brooks. I liked our chances
to win a medal, and I liked our team a lot, but what I found even more
surprising is that I liked Herb Brooks a lot more than I had previously.

Now, Herb was a friend, so it wasn't that I didn't like him and now
I did. No, in the twenty-two years that had passed, I knew that I had
changed, and I saw that Herb had changed, too. And it was for the better.

He was relaxed. He was at ease this time around, as before he had
always been so intense, which sometimes made you think twice about
approaching him. But he was not like that in 2002. He had matured as
a person and as a coach. He was sixty-five years old, and a grandfather,
and he told me that the real hero in his family—and I consider Herb an
American hero for what he did with the Olympic teams—was his wife,
Patti.

He said to me, "I have to give 100 percent credit to Patti. Sure, I
went to work and brought home the bacon. But she raised the kids. And
I missed out. However, now I have my grandkids and I'm having the time
of my life."

He was just so light-hearted and happy. It was a pleasure to be
around him. And I told him that he had become a different guy. He
actually bristled at that, in a good-natured way.

"Don't give me that bullshit, Lou!" he said. I told him it was true, and
that he should be proud of how he had developed as a coach and as a person. Believe me. As a divorced father of two, I knew the toll that hockey

could take on a family, and I told him he should be very happy that things were as he had described them, which I knew they were because I could see the change in him. He dismissed me again, but in a jocular way. I think he knew it was true but to admit it would be a sign that he had been, well, difficult at times, so he just smiled, and we kept going.

We went through the process of scouting players, and just as in 1980, Herb knew what he wanted, because he knew what we needed. A complete team, one that could skate, play a fast, creative game, or a strong physical game, and put pucks in the net. We needed a winner, and Herb picked that team.

Once again, Craig Patrick was with us, and I think he might be the most underrated contributor to our Olympic success in both 1980 and 2002. In 2002 he was the general manager of the Pittsburgh Penguins, and he knew the hockey world inside out, even if he had come off a couple of rough years in Pittsburgh, due to some trades that were heavily criticized—and not without merit for being so—and the team's financial woes. However, with the 2002 US Olympic men's hockey team, Craig was the glue that held us all together.

Craig was the perfect conduit between the players and Herb in his capacity as the Olympic team's general manager. He didn't care about credit. He just did his job.

We had a summer camp for the team for five days in Colorado Springs, to see how the team that we had selected fit together. I suggested that we should bring in the 1960 Olympic coach who won gold in Squaw Valley to come in and talk to the team. Herb had been the last player cut from that team and had to watch the team he had come so close to making now win gold without him. Herb would tell the coach, Jack Riley, after the Olympics, in complete sincerity and without bitterness, that Riley had clearly made the right call to cut him, as the team had won it all. It was a pivotal moment in Herb's own development as a coach.

So Jack Riley came out to Colorado Springs to meet the team. He was from Boston, and he was the type of guy who would have been leading the revolution against the British a couple of centuries earlier. When he came to see us in Colorado Springs in the summer of 2001, he had just turned eighty-one years old, but he still had the swagger of the athlete and the warrior he had been.

He had played hockey at Dartmouth before and after he served for four years as a navy pilot flying missions against the Japanese during World War II. Jack returned from the war, went back to Dartmouth, got a degree in economics in 1947, and then he played hockey for the United States in the 1948 Winter Olympics in St. Moritz, Switzerland. He came home and served as the head hockey coach at the US Military Academy in West Point, New York, from 1950 until 1986, where he was also the assistant athletic director. He won NCAA Coach of the Year twice, and he had been inducted into the International Ice Hockey Federation Hall of Fame in 1998.[1]

The team we had in Colorado Springs was made up entirely of pro players, as the Olympics had changed policy in 1986 to allow professional athletes to compete in the Olympics, starting in 1988. Even so, the NHL did not allow its players to compete until a decade later, figuring that allowing players to play in the Olympics would cause too long a break in the NHL season, which can already run into mid-June with the playoffs. The NHL overcame that concern in 1998, and Nagano was the first Olympic games where NHLers could play, where the Czechs took their revenge on the Russians and beat them for the gold.

So the 2002 Olympics were the second time that NHLers could play in the Games, and we made sure that we had taken the best. Some of them, like Chris Chelios, had played for me in the Olympics in 1984, and one of our goalies in 2002, Tom Barrasso, had nearly played for the United States in 1984, but he left us early for the NHL. Now they were both on the ice along with an all-star cast of NHL players.

Jack Riley was amused, a little bit, by how much things had changed. When he coached the US Olympic hockey team, professional players were forbidden to participate in all Olympic sports. Riley's 1960 US squad consisted of seventeen amateurs, all of whom came from Massachusetts or Minnesota because back in those days, they were the country's major hockey states. His players earned $7 a week and had to pay their own expenses. Four of his guys showed up for the training camp at West Point by paddling canoes up the Hudson River.

In 2002, some of our guys flew in on private jets. But they were all very keen to meet Jack Riley, and I was delighted to see him again.

I first met him when I was sixteen years old, when a team from Brooklyn tried to play a hockey team in West Point. We were horrible, but Riley was a gentleman about the whole thing and treated us as equals.

In 1979, I brought Anatoly Tarasov to West Point when I had Tarasov come over to the United States to do a hockey clinic tour. Jack Riley had been Tarasov's nemesis in 1960, because Riley had beaten Tarasov's Russian team on his way to winning the hockey gold medal. The Russians had left with bronze, and when Tarasov and Riley met each other again nearly twenty years later, they were smiling and happy and hugging each other, and then Tarasov said to Riley, "I want to thank you very much for getting me fired." Tarasov had been switched from head coach to an assistant after the Games in 1960, and he would never coach the team in another Olympic tournament. And he was just kidding. Riley and Tarasov had a great visit together.

I know that Jack appreciated what I did for him at USA Hockey. He had many grandchildren, and he would always call me and tell me he needed a dozen USA Hockey hats, or a bunch of jerseys, or some other USA Hockey merch. He would always try to pay, and I would never let him. He coached our national team in 1960 for nothing, and they won gold, so to charge the guy for any merch was just not going to happen. Over the years we had developed a tight friendship, and he was happy to come and speak to our next round of Olympic hockey players.

I know the players loved listening to Jack's stories, and Jack appreciated their attention and the respect they gave him. He didn't tell us that he was a war hero either, but I've heard that he did a lot of damage to the Japanese when he flew planes in the South Pacific in World War II. He knew everybody—from hockey players to presidents and generals. He liked to say that more US generals had played ice hockey than any other sport. For him, that meant they could only be the best.

He told the players to get out on the ice and play as hard and to work as hard and to fight as hard as they could. He told them that there was no greater honor than to play for your country, and they listened to a guy who had done it, and who had coached for decades at West Point.

Herb loved it, too, and just ate up this visit from his old coach, whom he adored, too.

The Winter Olympics began in February of 2002, and we were based in the Olympic Village in Salt Lake City. Herb and I arrived there three or four days before anybody else. We shared a college dorm room, which was fine, and we had a lot of free time.

Utah can be pretty nice even in the winter, and on days when the weather permitted, we were able to sit outside the dorm on a bench. We would talk about plans for the tournament, and what we needed to do, and the usual kind of pregame conversations that coaches have.

While Herb and I were sitting there one day, the Slovak coach, Jan Filtz, passed by us and I knew him well, so he stopped to say hello. I introduced him to Herb. I had coached a team that had beaten one of his teams in an international tournament the year before they beat us. They were a heck of a team, and he was a very talented coach. He could speak English fluently, and he sat with us on the bench, and we talked hockey for an hour.

He thought it was unfair that Slovakia didn't get an automatic hockey berth in the Olympics, and that they had to undergo a playoff round in one of two groups from countries then on the rise in the world of international hockey. We completely agreed with him, and so we talked about that. Herb got a kick out of it because he did not know a lot of hockey people internationally. He liked being introduced to them and having a visit with him.

In the previous winter Olympics, in Nagano in 1998, there had been an incident of vandalism caused by the US hockey team, which had blown up into an international mystery. The team never said who had thrown the broken deck furniture off the hotel balcony, but the media was still trying to find out. And they were asking me.

Herb had sent me to the first press conference because he didn't want to go. He knew what was coming. So I went along with players Brian Ralston and Bill Guerin, and there were some heavy media hitters in that auditorium. There were journalists from ABC, NBC, and CBS. I think Dan Rather was even there. They had come to put the screws to Herb

Brooks, and when they saw it was me who was in the coach's seat, they were all disappointed.

Herb just didn't want to deal with any of this. He said, "Lou, just be yourself. You'll say the right thing. You always do."

The first question I got was "What about the American team vandalism at the 1998 games in Nagano?"

I replied very matter-of-factly to that question, which I had expected, and said, "Here's what I know about it. Team USA defenseman Chris Chelios, who was also the captain, and who caused none of the damage, mailed a note of apology and a $3,000 check from his own pocket to cover repairs. I also know that they had lightweight furniture on the balcony. The Japanese are not usually as heavy as Americans, and some of our players were big, strong, heavy guys. And they sat on some of these chairs, and they broke like they were balsa wood or something; they just couldn't hold up the weight. And I also heard that some of the players threw chairs from the balcony down below into the snow, which was not a good thing. They've apologized. And that's all I know. That was then, and this is now, and it has been addressed."

They were not happy with this answer, and they kept at it. I got into it with the media in that room because I didn't like them. They were not real hockey journalists who had followed our team, which is something I would have respected. These were media stars who showed up because they thought that there was some salacious story to report that would make us look bad, and make Herb Brooks, the coach who won an Olympic gold medal, look bad, even though he and I were nowhere near the Nagano Games.

And there were people there who took mean shots at me going all the way back to Sarajevo in 1984, when I was the coach of the team that didn't follow the Miracle on Ice of 1980 with another miracle. They wrote some terrible things about me. I didn't say a word.

Nobody knew the real story and I wasn't going to tell them there. Nobody wanted to coach that team because they were afraid of failing after Herb and the guys won gold in 1980. That's why I ended up as coach, because somebody had to stand up no matter what.

We had excellent players in 1984, but they were young. Chris Chelios and Pat LaFontaine weren't even twenty years old. And we didn't play against the republic of this or that, we played against the Soviet Union, Czechoslovakia, Sweden, Finland, and Canada. And all of them had their very best players.

The Soviets and Czechs and Swedes and Finns had their best players because the NHL had not really opened up to them in 1984. In the 1983–1984 season, the players in the NHL were nearly 80 percent Canadian, nearly 13 percent American, and just under 4 percent Swedish.[2] But we could not take any of those American NHL players for our team in 1984, and some we wanted to take chose to sign with the NHL instead. I wasn't mad at any of them. I wasn't even disappointed. I probably would have done the same thing if I was offered big money and the NHL team had told me that they would play me right now in the NHL. It took the 1980 team's success to show the general managers in the NHL that the American kids can play. And we saw the results of American hockey development in the 2024 World Juniors, which were held in Sweden. Who won the gold medal? The kids from the United States.

Back in 2002, we saw a lot of good players on the rise from all over the world. Part of my job as an assistant coach was to see as many games featuring other teams as I could. So one day, Herb saw me getting ready to leave our dorm room in Salt Lake City, and he asked me where I was going. I told him I was going to Peaks Ice Arena, one of the Olympic hockey venues, which was in Provo, to watch the game between Austria and Germany who were playing a preliminary round game to try to advance to the final round. I wanted to scout them, and I especially wanted to see how the Germans played because they had a good team. I had a feeling they were going to make it into the final round.

Herb asked if he could come with me. I said, "Of course, that would be great," but that once I was at the rink, I was going to sit by myself and focus on the game. I didn't want to be distracted by having to talk to anybody sitting next to me. He understood.

Herb then wondered why we were leaving so early for this game, and I told him that the van we were driving in, like all vehicles going into Olympic sites, had to go through security. I told him that because of global terrorism, the Olympics were a target. Once we got there, I told him there would be dogs sniffing the van and security guys with mirrors on a long handle looking underneath our van to see if we had a bomb strapped to the bottom. This was all news to him, and I thought that he was going to change his mind, but he said he was up for it, so we went and got in the van.

I was happy he was going with me, as it would make the drive shorter, and we could talk hockey. I told Herb to put his seatbelt on. He said, no, he didn't wear a seatbelt. I said, "Herb, put your seatbelt on please. I'm responsible for the vehicle, I'm driving it. It's the law: you have to wear a seatbelt."

He shook his head and said that he refused to wear a seatbelt.

I told him to get out of the van. I said, "You're the coach of our hockey team. You tell me what you want me to do, and I will do it. I am 100 percent respectful. I need you to be respectful to me because I'm respectful of the law. So put the fucking seatbelt on or get out of the van."

He looked at me in surprise, then he made a comment which would one day come back to haunt me. He said, "You're worse than Patti," his wife, who apparently also had this issue with him. But he put the seatbelt on.

When we were about halfway to Provo, which is about a 45-minute drive south of Salt Lake City, I heard the "click" of a seatbelt being undone. I didn't say a word. I put my signal light on and pulled over to the side of the road. I said, "Get out. Hitchhike back. I'm not driving this van with you in it without your seatbelt on."

He clicked it back on and that was the end of that. We made it to Provo to watch the game.

It was a good game. Germany went up 2–0 in the first period, but the Austrians fought back to tie it in the second. Herb and I went to the snack bar to grab a coffee before what was promising to be an exciting third period, and we ran into Wayne Gretzky, who was the executive director of Canada's Olympic hockey in 2002, and Ken Hitchcock, who had been fired as the head coach of the Dallas Stars in 2001 and who was now an assistant coach to Team Canada. They were there scouting Germany, who they would wind up playing in a week's time.

We had just seen a very fine period. Two teams competing and playing hard. And showing some skill. And I remember Ken Hitchcock asked me what I thought of the game. I said, "It was a great period of hockey. I just loved it." And Hitchcock responded, "Yeah, if you like the American League."

The American League was a few rungs down from the NHL, and that was his lofty point. His team was much better than this. His lack of respect pissed me off. I said, "You don't think Germany can beat you?" He just rolled his eyes. So I said, "Let me tell you, every team should respect every team here. They might not have a hundred good players in their country, but they might have twenty, and we just saw those twenty. These two teams can play." And I walked away.

I went back to my seat for the third period, and I was fuming inside. Why didn't he respect these facts? I knew that his attitude also came with a big risk, as that kind of arrogance can blind you and cause you to lose. Which of course Canada nearly did when they played Germany. The first period was scoreless, and Canada scored three in the second. But the Germans roared back and got two in the third, and nearly tied it. Canada could have lost that game.

You cannot underrate your opponent or disrespect them. It's a major flaw that causes upsets. I wanted Germany to win that game, just to teach Canada a lesson. I used to tell Herb every day, "These teams are tougher. They're good. They can all play. Everybody can play."

He knew it. And he would remind the players by telling them not to take anything for granted. "We have to work and earn every shift to get every victory. Nothing is free."

And I said to myself, when are these Canadians going to learn to have more respect for other countries? We knew their disdain all too well as Americans. In the old days, it was often said that Canada controlled the NHL and that they kept American players out.

Now I worked as a scout with the Colorado Rockies and went to all the meetings where we assessed players, and we made our lists. And nothing could be further from the truth. The Canadians helped us a lot. And they still help us, for which I am grateful. They respect our players and coaches today, but twenty years ago, they did not have that degree of respect for anyone.

My job in 2002 was very much like what I had done in Lake Placid in 1980. I sat in the stands, high up, with a perfect view of the whole ice. Not far from me was the press box, with TVs, so I could look at something I wasn't sure of. When I came down to check in with Herb at intermission, I would try to keep Herb in a good and positive mood. I knew enough not to overdo it.

When I talked to my fellow assistant coach John Cuniff on the bench I would say simple things, as they could see the game too. I didn't want to clog up the line with chatter. One time I asked John if there was anything wrong with our forward, Chris Drury. I could see him ask Herb, and Herb shook his head no.

So I said, "Well, give him a shift." Some other guys were looking winded. So they put him on the ice, and he had a great shift. I noticed little simple things that you sometimes lose track of when you're on the bench.

We opened our Olympic schedule with a 6–0 victory over Finland. John LeClair scored three goals. In Nagano, Japan, we lost three of four games and LeClair scored no goals. This time we were playing on home ice, and I felt things were going to be different.

The ice was different too. It was bigger. Our NHLers had to adjust to the larger playing surface, which was 15 feet wider than the National Hockey League standard of 85 feet. With the bigger ice, there's more room for cross-ice passes, and the flow of the game is not up and down like in the smaller rinks of the NHL.

In fact, I will make a prediction that one day in the not-too-distant future, NHL rinks will get bigger. There are still two different rink sizes today in hockey. The NHL size is 200 feet long and 85 feet wide, which was the size of the rink that the world's first indoor hockey game was played on in Montreal in 1875, and it stuck. An Olympic rink is 200 feet long by 100 feet wide, and the blue lines are six feet further out from the goal, which makes the offensive zone even bigger.

I feel that because of the size of the players, we could probably avoid injuries if the rink was widened five to seven feet. The rinks in Europe and Asia are too big, and they slow down the game. Who doesn't want to see a player coming in on a two on one, taking a pass, and firing a slap shot? The goalie makes an unbelievable save but there's a rebound. The puck is bouncing around while players are fighting for control of it. Fans are on their feet, and it's great excitement. You don't want to see a player breezing around in the neutral zone, 20 feet away from everybody else, which is what you see on European and Asian rinks.

The rinks are too big when they're 100 feet wide. And they are a little too small at 85 feet. So let's compromise and make them 90 feet. If we do that, and I am confident that we shall, I think we will have a better game of hockey and one with fewer injuries.

The bigger ice was an issue for Canada's NHLers as well at the 2002 Olympics, and we saw that in their opener, which they lost to Sweden, 5–2. Then they barely beat the Germans, and they tied the Czechs 3–3.

We beat the Finns 6–0, tied the Russians 2–2, and then took care of Belarus 8–1. In the quarterfinals, Canada beat Finland 2–1, and Belarus 7–1. We beat Germany 5–0, and Russia 3–2. That was a tough game, and all of our goals were scored on the power play. The referee, the Canadian Bill McCreary, was one of the most respected in the NHL. Yet even before the game began, the Russians took issue with the officiating.

"It's hard to imagine how the judging can be of good quality and objective, given the fact that NHL judges live and work in North America," said Russia's president, Vladimir V. Putin, to reporters at the Kremlin, just a few hours before the puck drop.[3]

Our win against the Russians on February 22, 2002, came twenty-two years to the day after the Miracle on Ice when we beat the Soviet Union in the 1980 Games. The players were aware of it, and they were not out to duplicate the "miracle." They were trying to create their own legacy, and now they had a shot at winning the gold on home ice.

Of course, we did not know that Wayne Gretzky had the ice making crew, who were all Canadians, bury a Canadian loonie, which is their one-dollar coin, under center ice. So because we didn't know, it wasn't some kind of magic that we thought the Canadians used against us.

Herb was genuinely satisfied that the gold medal game came down to us versus Canada, the team against which we always had something to prove. I took my perch by myself up in the stands, as always, and had a TV nearby where I could watch replays of anything that I needed to see again. Although we took a 1–0 lead on a goal by Tony Amonte, I could see that the Canadians were fast, and I was impressed by how they never let up. Once Joe Sakic had put them ahead of us 3–2 late in the second period, that was it. We didn't score at all in the third, and Canada added two more to beat us 5–2.

Because they were the best. And they proved that by winning the gold medal. It wasn't the luck of that buried loonie. Although I felt if we had had Keith Tkachuk in our lineup, we might have had a shot. He was a fine, tough player who suffered a deep thigh bruise and pulled groin in the preliminary round and never played in the medal rounds. He could have made a difference.

But everyone could say that in every Olympics or every championship, those shoulda, coulda, wouldas. I always said that if my grandmother had balls, she would have been my grandfather. I think we could have won that gold medal in 2002, and we came very close. The effort was there. We just couldn't finish. So we took the silver medal, which is not that of the champion, but it's second best. On that day.

Something else happened on that day that was not good, and it need not have happened. I was standing outside our hospitality pavilion after the game with Herb when some executives from USA Hockey approached. One of them, and I won't say who, but it was one of the highest members of the organization, said, "Congratulations, Herb. Maybe you won't be making negative comments any more about the job we're doing at USA Hockey."

I could not believe it. The comment triggered Herb, and he said, "I'll say whatever I believe whenever I want."

He wanted to rant, so he asked me to take a walk with him, around a little lake that was there. "See what I mean?" he growled. "Those damn guys are not going to intimidate me. It's bullshit. Screw them. I'm not going to ever do anything else with USA Hockey as long as I live."

Here we go again, I thought. I reminded him of that story that Tarasov had told me. "I don't give a damn," he said. "I'm not giving in."

They didn't have to say that to Herb. We had just won a silver medal. The players did their best. Herb did a wonderful job. Yes, there's disappointment in losing the gold medal, but they should have just celebrated the moment. They should have just said, "Thank you, Herb. You did a great job. Thanks for everything you did." And left it at that.

I went back to Colorado Springs and went back to work at USA Hockey, and I tried to fix the damage they had done to Herb. I contacted Neil Sheehy, who was a member of the board of directors of USA Hockey. He was from Minnesota and had played in the NHL. He was also a very good friend of Herb's, and I thought he might be able to help get this very talented hockey man back on our team. Neil played an important role in getting Herb to coach in 2002, as well.

Herb was a very proud guy, and he was also stubborn. He told me that he appreciated everything that I had done for him, and for hockey, in the United States. "But don't try to convince me," he said. "Fool me once, shame on you. Fool me twice, shame on me. I was fooled twice and I'm not coming back."

It was one of the last things he ever said to me, as not long after that, he was gone. In August 2003, Herb was the director of player development for the Pittsburgh Penguins. He was driving a minivan back from a golf tournament in northern Minnesota that had raised money for the US Hockey Hall of Fame. He lost control of his minivan on an interstate highway, and he was thrown from the van when it rolled over.

There was no indication that Herb had been under the influence of anything other than fatigue. And he was not wearing his seatbelt.[4]

The night before his funeral, I went to the cathedral in Minnesota where Herb was laid out before his funeral Mass the next day. I waited in a long line to pass his body, as thousands of people had come to pay their respects to this American hero.

When I reached his casket, I said my prayers. Then I moved on, and saw Patti, Herb's wife, and she waved me over. All she said to me was, "You know, if only he had been wearing his seatbelt, he wouldn't be laid out in that casket."

And I knew exactly what she meant. Because that night when I drove down to Provo with Herb refusing to wear his seatbelt came rushing back into my mind. I knew she was right. If he had been wearing the seatbelt he would not have been thrown from the vehicle. That's what killed him. And now, there was nothing more to say.

I was working in my office at USA Hockey one day when my ex-wife Joni came in. She had driven up from Taos, New Mexico, because she couldn't tell me on the phone. She was just staring straight ahead, but she had cried, and her eyes were glassy. I knew why she was there. I said, "Greg is dead." She said yes.

I was stunned. I just sat quietly at my desk. I didn't know what to say. We went into the executive director's office, and Dave Ogrean was kind and generous. He gave us space.

We lost our youngest son Greg as a direct result of a mental illness. We don't know if he was murdered, or if he committed suicide; both are big possibilities. It happened in 2011 on a Native American reservation in Taos, New Mexico. He might have stopped taking his medication, and something happened. The police could not do any further investigation because the reservation is a sovereign nation. He was found hanging from a tree, and he either hanged himself, or someone killed him. Was he involved in the sale of drugs or something else? We don't know. We'll never know.

But something good came out of it. Joni and Dave came up with a plan to help Brian, our surviving son, who had also battled depression. And Joni said instead of people sending things, like flowers and cards, maybe they could make a contribution to the foundation we would start for Brian. We had spent all our money on the kids' health, and we had no more money. Maybe with a foundation, Brian could go to college. So that's what we did.

The NHL, and colleagues of mine at work, all contributed money. Vladislav Tretiak sent $16,000. We were so surprised we called him to make sure he meant to do so. He did. "This is what we do for our friends in hockey," he said. In the end we raised a nice chunk of money, and Brian did go to college.

Today, Joni and I share our one surviving son, Brian, and we only want the best for him, but we still love them both, even though Greg is gone. You still have to live. You can't collapse and give up on life.

So I plunged back into my work at USA Hockey. I am very proud of what I had accomplished in terms of how hockey had developed in the United States while I was working to do that very thing.

The director of player development for USA Hockey at the time was visiting our office, and he was frustrated. He said, "Lou, give me your honest opinion. What do we have to do to get better?"

At that time, we had no money. I never thought we should do anything extravagant. So I sat there and thought, and then I said, "Outside of Canada, which two countries have been the most successful at hockey? Czechoslovakia and the Soviet Union."

I laid out that the Czechs had an army program in Prague. And the Soviets had their army program in Moscow. Both teams had the best players in the country. The majority of the players play for the best coaches all year long, and they made up the heart of the national team. Their national teams were together 70 percent of the year. If we could get that kind of time with our very best young players, we would have an advantage in international hockey.

We would need to get sixty kids together for two months in the summer and bring them out to the training center. Were they willing to give up their summers? I didn't know. Could we afford it? I didn't know. But I knew that's what we had to do. And that's what we did.

Because of that, today we have thousands of qualified coaches. We have players from all over the country. When I started in 1979, the first world hockey summit was a major success in Boston, and since then there have been all kinds of world events. I came up with that idea and made it happen. It took twenty years after that before you saw the results, but those results are there.

It was one of the reasons that I got a big surprise in 2014. My boss came in and said, "I have an announcement to make, and I wanted to tell you first in person. You've been elected to the USA Hockey Hall of Fame. I was on the call, and it was unanimous."

I was humbled. I had never imagined myself in any Hall of Fame all those years ago on the roller hockey rinks in Brooklyn, but there I was in Minnesota, on December 6, 2014, being elevated to the pantheon. I did not write a speech, I just spoke from the heart, and told them a lot of the story that I have told you here. But in 10 minutes.

I did tell them a hockey joke that I want to share, as it still makes me laugh. Here's what I said:

Every time I come to Minnesota, it reminds me of two friends I had. They were old, retired goalkeepers, Billy and John. And they were in their eighties. And they'd go to the park every day, feed the squirrels peanuts and bread, and talk about the great old days when we played. "Don't you wish we could still be playing?" "Well, we can't, we're in our eighties. And we've come to the end of the line."

"Do you think there's hockey in heaven?" Bill said to John, and John said, "Geez, I don't know. That's a good question." So they reach an agreement. Whichever one dies first will come back as a spirit and tell the other one yes or no.

Well, a couple of years later, Bill dies, and John is depressed and lonely and feeding squirrels and sitting there by himself in the park. And he hears a voice. "Pssst. Pssst."

"Who is it?"

"You big dummy. You can't see me. It's Bill. I'm a spirit." He said, "Listen, I got good news and bad news for you."

"What is it?"

"What do you want first?"

John says give me the good news.

"Well, there is hockey in heaven. Fastest game you'll ever see. Nobody ever gets injured. Beautiful ice palaces. Sometimes even God comes to a game. It's fantastic."

John said, "That's great. What could the bad news be?"

"You're starting in goal tomorrow night."

CHAPTER 13

Back Behind the Bench

AFTER I LEFT USA HOCKEY A COUPLE OF YEARS AGO, I DIDN'T KNOW what I was going to do. In truth, I didn't leave; I was asked to get out.

Now I had been there for the better part of forty years and counting, and when I hit my seventies, I asked the executive director, Dave Ogrean, if he wanted me to go. And if they did, I asked if they would come up with a retirement program like they did with other guys with whom I had worked. Art Berglund received a $50,000-a-year pension, and he had been the general manager of a couple of US Olympic hockey teams and had joined USA Hockey in 1996. So nearly twenty years after me. I figured I rated at least as much. But Dave said no, keep coming in to work, they loved having me around, and so I did.

When Pat Kelleher became executive director of USA Hockey in 2017, I was happy. He came from an esteemed hockey family. His late father, Dan, had coached youth hockey in Belmont, Massachusetts, for forty years. In 2001, we gave him the William Thayer Tutt Award, USA Hockey's highest volunteer honor.

I approached Pat three different times and said, "Pat, I'm getting up there in age. Do you still want me to come in?"

He asked if I liked coming in, and I said yes, so he told me to keep coming in. He asked if I still wanted to come in, and I said that I did. When I reached age seventy-five, I asked him if I should still come in. He said yes. I stayed because I saw many of the programs that I had started had been getting better and better, and it fueled me. I loved to help make USA Hockey and hockey in the United States grow.

My responsibilities had diminished, but I liked working and I never missed a day. I took it upon myself to manage the building. I would help the interns who would come onboard by getting them chairs or tables or microwaves and making sure they were alright. I was the house manager.

Then one day, a couple of years ago, Pat asked me to come into his office. He was beet red, and he told me that I wasn't contributing that much anymore, and they needed to make room for new people, and there was a pandemic still going on, and as a result, they were "discontinuing" my position.

I said, "How about I discontinue your face with rights and lefts?" In my book, that's being fired. He said I wasn't being fired, but that made it even worse.

No, what made it even worse was when they offered me such a ridiculously low compensation that I am too embarrassed to even mention it, and they invoked the pandemic as justification for that, even though they had $44 million in their foundation. I just found out that a kid I had brought in to work at USA Hockey from a golf course in Minnesota was making $290,000 a year plus bonuses.

And they knew I was in financial straits because I had spent so much money helping my kids, who suffered so badly from depression. I had used everything in my 401K to pay for my sons' medical care, and that fund was empty.

They fired a bunch of us that day, a real St. Valentine's Day Massacre, and before I left someone said I should speak to Karen Hackman, whose husband, Tom, our receptionist, was also let go, but she stayed on. I can only imagine that night's dinner conversation. She told me to get on this thing called COBRA for my health insurance, and I had just enough money in my account to do it.

It's a good thing I did. Because even though I was seventy-six years old and I had never been ill, or had surgeries, or anything like that, just a week after I was told that my health insurance was done like my job was done, I was in the hospital with a prostate problem that nearly did me in. And even with COBRA, it ended up costing me $16,000 in bills. Talk about adding injury to insult.

This was the first time in my life that I had been fired. I had never even been reprimanded. I have never complained about being let go. They have a right to replace me. I was seventy-six years old, and it was time for fresh blood. I felt privileged to work in USA Hockey. And remember, I was the fourth-ever employee there. But it was the way they made me leave that was so insulting. If this is their idea of a thank you, well, I can only hope that karma remembers that when it's time for them to leave.

Pat Kelleher is not a bad man, but he could make things right with me while we're still on planet Earth. However, let's just say that thought is kind of like pulling your goalie when you're down by three goals with fifteen minutes left in the game and thinking you can win. Beyond optimistic.

However, hockey did not desert me, nor did I desert it. Andrew Sherman, who owns the Monument Rink and the Rampage program, at which I now teach, got me back in the game. Hailing from Schenectady, New York, Andrew played college hockey with the Rochester Institute of Technology Tigers, then became an NHL player agent from 1998 to 2003.

After he was done as a player agent, he came out to Colorado Springs. He came to the USA Hockey office and asked to speak to somebody about getting involved in youth hockey. Tom Hackman, the receptionist who was let go with me in the massacre, buzzed me and said, "There's a guy down here who wants to get involved in coaching and hockey. Would you be interested in talking to him?" I said sure. I had never turned anyone away from hockey in my life and was not about to start.

Andrew was a very friendly, thoughtful man, and he wanted to start coaching a youth hockey team. I met with him for an hour. I had talked to him about the importance of off-ice training, and offered all the information I had: videos and a coaching manual that I had put together. I wished him well and very much hoped he would establish his program for kids.

One day I looked out the window of my office, and in the park across the street I saw a bunch of kids jumping and running through cones and doing what looked like dryland training for hockey. I walked over to see what was up, and I was delighted to see that it was Andrew's team of kids in action.

He kept going with his plan to develop youth hockey in this part of the world, and as a result, he bought twin roller hockey rinks out of bankruptcy in Monument, Colorado, and turned them into ice rinks. He has developed a wonderful program for hockey players of all ages, with a talented staff of dedicated coaches. He even managed to produce a player who made it to the NHL: Brandon Carlo, who is today a defenseman for the Boston Bruins.

They also have many kids who came through their program and then went on to play college hockey, minor league hockey, and hockey in Europe. Andrew created an excellent program for kids to learn the beauties of hockey in a safe and respectful place.

When I got fired by USA Hockey, Andrew checked in with me to see how I was doing. I told him I was managing, but I was dealing with this prostate issue that was going to require surgery. He asked me how I was doing financially. "Do you need any money, Lou?"

I most certainly did, but I am a proud guy, so I said no, I was fine. "But I'm going to need to supplement my Social Security income because I can't live on that alone."

So anyway, he invited me to join his coaching staff. He doesn't rip people off and charge outlandish fees, so I am not making a fortune, but I get by.

I also worked at the zoo for a while. My neighbor was an elephant keeper at the beautiful zoo we have here in Colorado Springs. She got me an interview with the boss, and I got a gig running the carousel for a few months. The pay was little, but the fun was large.

I worked at the carousel three days a week, eight hours a day, but as time went on, I couldn't continue because I wasn't physically able to hoist the little kids onto the carousel horses. It wasn't safe for them or for me.

That's when I decided to stick with the hockey at Andrew's Rampage program. It helps the reputation of his place to have a former Olympic and NHL coach join his excellent team of coaches who all have their fine pedigrees and do a wonderful job with the kids.

Andrew lets me do my own thing. Last year I coached a bantam double A team, which was a real joy. This year I'm doing off-ice training specifically for hockey. I've been working mostly with kids aged ten and under. The results have been great. They don't miss a session unless they're sick. They have a lot of fun, and I have a lot of fun.

I work closely with the coaches who coach these kids on ice. The on-ice coaches are amazed at their agility and their explosive skating. These young players are really keen to be their best, and we're helping them to do that.

The key with me is that I have to love what I am doing or I don't do it. And I love what I'm doing. And the kids know that, and so they love what they're doing.

I am bad with names, so I have created a system that helps me to remember and makes it even more fun for them. I give them nicknames because they want nicknames. I have one player named Everett, so his nickname is Mount Everest. I have another I call Chicken McNuggets, and it turned out that this was his favorite food.

Now, at training, I'll ask, "What's your name?" And they never tell me their real name. They tell me their nickname, and I remember who they are. Some of the parents have told me that the nicknames are so popular the kids want to be called that name at home. It's all they will answer to. Chicken McNuggets has his nickname written on his bedroom door.

When I first started coaching with Andrew, part of me expected these kids to be very different from the ones I had coached many years ago in Flushing, Queens. I thought they would be spoiled, not in a useless way, but in an entitled way.

I found out to my surprise how wonderful these kids are. They're very smart. People keep telling me that the school systems are falling apart. These are smart kids. I used the word "infinity" to them. I think that no nine-year-old knows what infinite or infinity means. So I asked them if they knew and every hand in the room went up. And the hands keep going up no matter what I ask, but I only ask questions that I know the answer to, so there's nothing in my question arsenal about the intricacies of nuclear fusion.

They're not only smart, but they're kind to each other, and to me. I run some tough, demanding workouts, but I treat them with respect. I tell them, "Make sure you hydrate. If you have to use the men's room, or ladies' room"—we have girls playing too, and it's wonderful to have this mixed classroom—"you don't even have to tell me. Just take off and come back as soon as you're done. Your health comes first, and your needs come first." They hate that they have to go to the bathroom because they know they are missing something that might be fun.

They do things for me all the time. I hand them my phone and ask them to find out something for me that we need to know for our workout. And they're off, their hands flying over the phone keys, and they have the answer for me in seconds.

They are also very responsible. When I first started working with them outside a couple of summers ago, every once in a while, I'd have to blow the whistle or shout just to get their attention. They could be in the middle of anything, and a siren would sound, or a truck would backfire, and their heads would look in that direction. Their attention spans are the attention spans of kids.

I said to myself, don't become a drill sergeant. Don't rely on the whistle. Rely on them. Let the kids take responsibility. So now, if their attention wanders, I just stop talking and fold my arms and look at them. And those kids who were looking somewhere else or whispering to each other come back to the group and pay attention.

They police themselves. I don't have to blow whistles and yell at them, and I have conveyed this to some of the other coaches, who have adopted it, too. If we let them take care of their own discipline, we will have a much better relationship with them. And we do.

Which is not to say we take it easy. A lot of the drills we do are very competitive, because if you don't compete, you'll never be a hockey player. I tell them, "There's a difference, guys, between losing and being beaten. You can get beat by a better opponent. And if you played hard, you can say that you competed, and you did everything that you could do. You were beaten by a better team, and that's okay, that's honorable. But it's never okay to lose. Losing means you didn't try, and that you didn't give your best effort."

But these kids always give their best effort. I always end my training session with a tug of war. I get the parents involved, too, and make them anchors. So there is a mother holding the rope and the kids are pulling and yanking and yelling and competing. And they learn to be good sportsmen. They have to give their due to the victor and work that much harder and smarter for the next competition, and they get it.

And then, two minutes after losing in a tug of war, a mother might say to her son, "Hey Chicken McNuggets, how about a hot chocolate?" And off they go for the drink, forgetting that they just lost tug of war. This is good and healthy and normal. This is how it should be, a balance between life and sport. These kids invigorate me. They do more for me than I do for them.

Even though Andrew keeps his program affordable, you still have to be middle or upper middle class to afford it. That's one reason we started the foundation in my name. As I did back in Flushing, Queens, I want to help any kid who wants to play hockey to play hockey.

Hockey sticks alone can cost $250. When I was playing, I bought my first brand-new stick, a Northland Pro, in 1955 from a shop at Madison Square Garden. It cost me $2. So today the Lou Vairo Foundation's purpose is to support and strengthen youth hockey in southern Colorado. Our goal is to raise money to provide grants and scholarships for programs and players who need a little help.

And we have had deep support. Recently a player who played for me in 1976–1977 sent me a text message to say that he donated $5,000 to the foundation. His text said, "You did a lot for me coach. I know this is a good cause. I never forgot the life lessons, not just hockey lessons. I'll be forever grateful. Mike." It's very moving to me to see how players with whom I have shared the game now want to use their resources to share it with others.

I was at a dinner not too long ago in a house that was built by a former college hockey player, in a very exclusive area of town. He played hockey at Colorado College, then went into construction and created a very successful business. He and his wife built this magnificent house on a hill overlooking the Garden of the Gods. It's the most beautiful view in the world.

I was admiring his house and looking at the gorgeous marble fixtures. He told me that he made a special trip to Tuscany, Italy, to go to the quarry where Michelangelo got his marble. "Have you ever heard of Carrera?" he asked.

I said, "Yeah. We had a hockey training camp about two miles from there."

He asked me about my hockey time in Italy and I told him, and then I told him about what I was up to now in Colorado Springs. He was very interested and wanted to know more. Like everyone, the more people hear about what we do, the more they want to help.

Bob Naglee was also there at this dinner, and he used to own the Minnesota Wild. And he's a very rich man. He's on the USA Hockey Foundation Board. I said, "I'm going to ask the USA Hockey Foundation to donate a million dollars to kids in southern Colorado for hockey."

And he said, "Well, good luck. I'm happy to propose it."

I said, "They screwed me over and they don't have to give me anything, but I want them to give my foundation money. It's tax-deductible."

"How about I start with a check right now?" He said, "For five grand?"

I said, "I am happy to take it." It was a lucrative night for the foundation as we took in about $15,000 in donations and generated a lot of goodwill for it. And that's what I have for hockey.

I feel happy to be in the hockey world again. Having stood behind the bench in Lake Placid and in Sarajevo, in Madison Square Garden, and in the Montreal Forum and Maple Leaf Gardens, I can't wait for Monday, Tuesday, Wednesday nights when the kids I coach today play on their teams. I showed up last week and the coach said, "Coach Lou, come on the bench." There's no difference to me from standing in those great hockey palaces to standing on outside turf or inside the gym, or behind a bench with these little guys who want to play hockey. If I am the godfather of anything, let it be that I am the godfather of their hockey dreams, seasoned with my own, going forward. It's the only direction I want to go. To play the game is great. To win the game is greater. To love the game is the greatest of them all.

NOTES

CHAPTER 1

1. Dollar Times, https://www.dollartimes.com/inflation/inflation.php?amount=1.45 &year=1950.

2. Ticketmaster, https://www.ticketmaster.com/event/1D005F26C50047C7 ?tfl=New_York_Yankees-Tickets-Yankees_Individual_Game_Tickets _for_April_19,_2024-Ticket_Grid_Buy_Now_Button-x0-Desktop -Landscape&adobe_mc=MCMID=1569391529130728468257587648665420977 9&MCORGID=A65F776A5245B01B0A490D44%40AdobeOrg&TS=1713457427&affiliateId =tdl-New_York_Yankees-Tickets-Buy_Yankees_Tickets-Single_Game_Tickets_Buy _Tickets_Button-x0-Desktop- =.

3. Off the Leash, https://offtheleash.net/2023/06/04/growing-up-in-the-50s-nedicks/.

CHAPTER 2

1. "Messina Earthquake," American Experience, PBS.org, https://www.pbs.org/wgbh/ americanexperience/features/rescue-messina-earthquake/.

2. "Battlefield: Vietnam," PBS.org, https://www.pbs.org/battlefieldvietnam/timeline/ index1.html.

CHAPTER 3

1. Tobias Stark and Hart Cantelon, "Guru or Court Jester? The Lloyd Percival Paradox: The Globalization of Training Regimes—The Case of Canada, Sweden and the Soviet Union," *Sport in Society* 23, no. 3 (2020): 539–56, https://www.tandfonline.com/ doi/full/10.1080/17430437.2020.1696540.

2. Lloyd Percival, *The Hockey Handbook*, revised by Wayne Major and Robert Thom (Toronto: McClelland & Stewart, 1993), first published 1951, https://archive.org/details /hockeyhandbook00lloy/page/12/mode/2up.

CHAPTER 4

1. The Mike Buckna information comes from Michael McKinley, *Hockey: A People's History* (Toronto: McClelland & Stewart, 2006), 120–24.

CHAPTER 5

1. "Chilly Breeze from Moscow," *New York Times*, June 13, 1970, https://www.nytimes.com/1970/06/13/archives/chilly-breeze-from-moscow.html?searchResultPosition=70.

CHAPTER 6

1. Dollar Times, https://www.dollartimes.com/inflation/inflation.php?amount=12&year=1978.

2. Dollar Times, https://www.dollartimes.com/inflation/inflation.php?amount=9000&year=1978.

3. Dollar Times, https://www.dollartimes.com/inflation/inflation.php?amount=10000&year=1978.

4. Jim Kaplan, "Young Blades," *Sports Illustrated*, February 9, 1976, https://vault.si.com/vault/1976/02/09/young-blades.

5. *Wall Street Journal* staff, "Does Stretching Prevent Exercise Injuries?," YouTube, December 3, 2014, https://www.youtube.com/watch?v=6bdL5qpNFt8.

CHAPTER 7

1. "1979 National Sports Festival—Colorado Springs," Vintage Minnesota Hockey, https://history.vintagemnhockey.com/page/show/8110780-1979-national-sports-festival-colorado-springs.

2. Ibid.

3. Information about the Patricks comes from Michael McKinley, *Hockey: A People's History* (Toronto: McClelland & Stewart, 2006), 64–70.

4. "1979–80 NHL Schedule and Results," Hockey Reference, https://www.hockey-reference.com/leagues/NHL_1980_games.html.

CHAPTER 11

1. The actual number of active Black players is currently thirty-four. See Ankit Kumar, "How Many Black Players Are in the NHL?," Sportskeeda, modified June 3, 2023, https://www.sportskeeda.com/ice-hockey/news-how-many-black-players-nhl.

2. See Michael McKinley, *Willie: The Game-Changing Story of the NHL's First Black Player* (New York: Viking, 2020), 207.

CHAPTER 12

1. US Hockey Hall of Fame, "John P. 'Jack' Riley, Jr. Bio," https://www.ushockeyhalloffame.com/page/show/820417-john-p-jack-riley-jr-; Marvin Pave, "Jack Riley, 95; Coached First US Hockey Team to Win Olympic Gold," *Boston Globe*, 1960, https://epaper.bostonglobe.com/BostonGlobe/article_popover.aspx?guid=6e23282c-79f7-4442-a4b6-b37473bc51fe&source=next.

2. "NHL Totals by Nationality: 1983–1984 Stats," QuantHockey, https://www.quanthockey.com/nhl/nationality-totals/nhl-players-1983-84-stats.html.

3. Joe Lapointe, "Russia Questions Officials from North America," *New York Times*, February 23, 2002, https://www.nytimes.com/2002/02/23/olympics/russia-questions-officials-from-north-america.html.

4. Associated Press, "Herb Brooks Fell Asleep before Fatal Crash," Minnesota Public Radio, September 16, 2003, https://news.minnesota.publicradio.org/features/2003/09/16_ap_brookscrash/.

INDEX

Photospread images are indicated by *p1, p2, p3,* etc.

About the Authors

Lou Vairo has been at the forefront in the development of hockey in the United States for parts of the last six decades. In the 1960s, Vairo was a leader in building grassroots hockey programs in New York City. He transitioned to coaching in the 1970s, highlighted by a 1976 national championship while directing the Austin (Minn.) Mavericks of the US Hockey League. It was Vairo who is widely credited for bringing European concepts of training and playing to the United States in the early 1970s, including methods learned when he studied under Soviet coach Anatoly Tarasov.

Vairo served as head coach of the US National Junior Team from 1979 to 1982, and once again in 2003. He played a significant role as a scout for the 1980 US Olympic Men's Ice Hockey Team that captured the gold medal in Lake Placid, New York. After serving as the head coach of the 1984 US Olympic Men's Ice Hockey Team, Vairo went to the NHL's New Jersey Devils where he was an assistant coach for two seasons.

On five occasions (1983, 2000–2003), Vairo was head coach of the US Men's National Team. Vairo also was an assistant coach of the silver medal–winning 2002 US Olympic Men's Ice Hockey Team, helping guide Team USA to its first Olympic medal in twenty-two years.

In addition to his contributions in the United States, Vairo also influenced hockey abroad. He served as head coach of the Dutch National Team, head coach of HC Milano in Italy, and head coach of HC Milano Saima in Italy, guiding the team to the 1991 Italian League National Championship.

Vairo became the fourth full-time member of the Amateur Hockey Association of the United States (now USA Hockey) staff in 1978 and served as director of special projects for USA Hockey beginning in 1992. Vairo led the creation of the Diversity Task Force and what are known today as USA Hockey Player Development Camps. He has also been widely involved in the USA Hockey's Coaching Education Program

Vairo was inducted into the US Hockey Hall of Fame in 2014, honored by the IIHF with the Paul Loicq Award in 2010, and received the NHL's Lester Patrick Trophy in March 2000. Vairo was honored twice in 1994 for his lifetime commitment to hockey, receiving both the John "Snooks" Kelley Founders Award from the American Hockey Coaches Association and the Walter Yaciuk Award from USA Hockey.

Michael McKinley is a journalist, author, screenwriter, and filmmaker. He was educated at the University of British Columbia and at Oxford University.

Michael has written many books, both as the sole author and as a collaborator. One of his most recent, which he wrote with Willie O'Ree, is *Willie: The Game-Changing Story of the NHL's First Black Player*, which was named one of the Top 20 Books of 2020 by the CBC and nominated for a 2021 NAACP Image Award. He cowrote *A Quiet Life*, a cybercrime thriller, with Will Cooper, 2024; *The Glamor of Evil*, a spy thriller novel, with Nancy Merritt Bell, 2024; *Ice Capades: A Memoir of Fast Living and Tough Hockey*, with Sean Avery, 2014; and *The Codebreakers: The Secret Intelligence Unit that Changed the Course of the First World War*, with James Wyllie. He is currently cowriting *Party Crasher: How Jesse Ventura Changed Politics in America*, with Riley Rinehart, and has just completed the memoir *Diamond Dust* with Russ Swain, 2024.

For TV and film, his most recent projects are *Epstein's Shadow: Ghislaine Maxwell*, cocreator and co-executive producer of the three-part series, 2021; *Let's Do a Miracle*, a forthcoming feature documentary created with Elissa Montanti, Alice Barrett Mitchell, and Nancy Bell, which McKinley wrote, directed, and produced; *Lincoln's Law*, a TV drama series, created with Mark Hoeger; *Dead Right*, a TV drama series; *Hot Springs*, a feature film, with Michael Sofranko; *Singers Anonymous*, a TV reality series, created with Julia Amisano; co-executive producer of the one-hour TV documentary *Engraved on a Nation: Man versus Machine*, 2019; created, cowrote, and produced *The Two Marys*, winner of the Gracie Award for Best Hour-long Documentary aired in the United States.

As a journalist, he has written for many newspapers and magazines, and has won national news and magazine writing awards. He is a citizen of Canada, Ireland, and the United States and lives in Brooklyn, New York. Please see www.libertayo.com for a digital sampling of Michael McKinley's work.